SUTTON POCKET HISTORIES

THE CIVIL WARS
1637–1653

MARTYN BENNETT

SUTTON PUBLISHING

First published in the United Kingdom in 1998 by
Sutton Publishing Limited · Phoenix Mill
Thrupp · Stroud · Gloucestershire · GL5 2BU

British Library Cataloguing in Publication Data
A catalogue record for this book is available from the British
Library.

ISBN 0-7509-1912-4

Cover picture : detail from An Eyewitness Representation of the
Execution of King Charles I of England, 1649 *by Weesop (private
collection/photograph, Bridgeman Art Library, London)*

 ^{TM} ALAN SUTTON™ and SUTTON™ are the
trade marks of Sutton Publishing Limited

Typeset in 11/14 pt Baskerville.
Typesetting and origination by
Sutton Publishing Limited.
Printed in Great Britain by
The Guernsey Press Company Limited,
Guernsey, Channel Islands.

Contents

For Deborah

Acknowledgements

I would like to thank the Faculty of Humanities at Nottingham Trent University for allowing me a period of sabbatical leave in 1998 during which I was able to work on this book, and other projects. I also wish to thank Dr Deborah Tyler-Bennett for reading through the drafts of this book and for her invaluable comments and suggestions.

List of Dates

28 August. The king's army is defeated at Newburn and twelve English peers petition the king for a new Parliament at Westminster.

3 November. The Long Parliament meets.

11 November. Root and Branch Petition presented to Parliament, and the Earl of Strafford is arrested.

21 November. The Archbishop of Canterbury is arrested.

1641 **May**. The Army plot to rescue the Earl of Strafford is exposed.

12 May. Strafford is executed.

14 August. Charles arrives in Edinburgh to ratify the Treaty of London.

October. The Incident is exposed.

22 October. Rebels seize strongholds across Ulster.

23 November. The *Grand Remonstrance* is sent to the king by the Westminster Parliament and published.

1642 **5 January**. Charles fails to arrest six of his leading opponents.

11 March. The Militia Ordinance gives control of the militia to Parliament.

22 April. The king is refused entry into Hull.

May. The king begins issuing Commissions of Array to regain control of the militia.

22 August. The king raises his standard at Nottingham.

23 September. Royalists win the battle of Powick Bridge.

October. The Confederation of Kilkenny assembles.

23 October. The battle of Edgehill.

12–13 November. The king fails to advance on London.

1643 **23 February**. The queen returns from Europe with arms and ammunition for the royalists.

March–April. Peace negotiations held at Oxford.

30 June. Royalists win the battle of Adwalton Moor.

September. The Cessation ends fighting between the Confederation and the government forces in Ireland.

September. The Westminster Parliament allies with the Scots in the Solemn League and Covenant.

6 September. The Earl of Essex relieves Gloucester.

20 September. Parliamentarians win the first battle of Newbury.

1644 **January**. The king opens an alternative Parliament at Oxford.

16 January. The Scottish Army of the Solemn League and Covenant invades England.

29 March. Parliamentarians win the battle of Cheriton.

11 April. Parliamentarians win the battle of Selby.

19 June. The battle of Cropredy Bridge.

June. Alasdair MacColla and 1,600 Irish troops land in Scotland.

1 July. Prince Rupert relieves York.

2 July. Scots and parliamentarians win the battle of Marston Moor.

August. The Marquis of Montrose joins forces with MacColla.

1 September. Montrose defeats Covenanter forces at Tippemuir in Scotland. Essex's army surrenders to Charles at Lostwithiel.

13 September. Royalists win the battle of Justice Mills, Aberdeen.

18 September. Parliamentarians win the battle of Montgomery.

26 October. The second battle of Newbury.

1645 **February**. The New Model Army is created.

2 February. Royalists win the battle of Inverlochy.

April. The Self-Denying Ordinance is passed by the House of Lords.

9 May. Royalists win the battle of Auldearn.

31 May. Royalists capture Leicester.

14 June. Parliamentarians win the battle of Naseby.

2 July. Royalists win the battle of the Bridge of Alford.

10 July. Parliamentarians win the battle of Langport.

1 August. Parliamentarians win the battle of Colby Moor.

15 August. Royalists win the battle of Kilsyth.

13 September. Covenanter Scots win the battle of Philliphaugh.

23 September. Parliamentarians win the battle of Rowton Heath.

1 November. Parliamentarians win the battle of Mold.

1646 **January**. Charles's secret treaty with the Kilkenny government is exposed and repudiated.

3 February. Chester surrenders to the parliamentarians.

21 March. Parliamentarians win the battle of Stow-on-the-Wold.

5 May. Charles surrenders to the Scots besieging Newark.

5 June. Confederation forces win the battle of Benburb.

July. Parliament presents Charles with the Newcastle Propositions.

4 August. Treaty between Ormond and Kilkenny published by the Confederation.

1 September. Ormond Treaty repudiated by the Papal nuncio, Rinuccini and Owen Roe O'Neill.

1647 **30 January**. The Scots hand Charles over to Parliament.

March. The radical political group the Levellers circulates the Large Petition.

April. Regiments of the horse begin to elect

representatives known as Agitators to campaign for back pay and a new social settlement.

4 June. Cornet Joyce seizes the king from Holdenby House.

14 June. The army marches on London.

19 June. Ormond leaves Ireland and hands Dublin to Michael Jones and parliamentarian forces.

23 July. The army leaders present the *Heads of the Proposals* to the king.

26 July. Riots in London force Parliament to oppose the army.

4 August. The army occupies outer London.

8 August. Parliamentarians win the battle of Dungan's Hill in Leinster.

October–November. Radical proposals put forward by the army and by the Levellers are debated at Putney.

11 November. Charles escapes.

13 November. Parliamentarian forces win the battle of Knocknanuss in Munster.

15 November. Mutiny at Ware.

24 December. Charles rejects the Four Bills presented to him by Parliament, already having signed the Engagement with the Scots.

25 December. Riots at Canterbury, London and Norwich because of the abolition of Christmas.

1648   **22 February**. Governor John Poyer refuses to hand Pembroke to New Model Army forces, beginning a rebellion in Wales.

10 April. Poyer declares his support for the king.

28 April. Scots seize Berwick upon Tweed.

8 May. Welsh rebels defeated at St Fagans.

11 May. Rebellion in Kent.

30 May–1 June. Kentish rebels defeated by Fairfax.

4 June. Rebellion breaks out in Essex. The rebels there are joined by fleeing Kentish rebels.

5 June. Rebels in North Wales defeated at Y Daler Hir.

20 June. Fairfax besieges Essex and Kentish rebels in Colchester.

8 July. The Engager army invades north-west England.

11 July. Pembroke Castle surrenders to Cromwell, ending the rebellion in South Wales.

17 August. Parliamentarians win the battle of Preston.

29 August. Colchester surrenders to Parliament.

26 September. The Engager government collapses.

1 October. Rebellion in North Wales crushed on Anglesey.

6 November. Pride's Purge.

1649   **19 January**. Ormond and the Confederation establish a new treaty.

21 January. Trial of Charles begins at Westminster.

27 January. Charles is sentenced to death.

30 January. Charles is executed at Whitehall.

10 February. Charles's son proclaimed King Charles II.

17 March. The monarchy is abolished.

19 March. The House of Lords is abolished.

1 April. Digger colonies are established.

25 April and 5 May. Women's petitions for the release of Leveller prisoners are presented to Parliament.

15 May. Leveller mutiny put down at Burford.

2 August. Parliamentarian forces win the battle of Rathmines.

11 September. Cromwell storms Drogheda.

12 October. Cromwell storms Wexford.

1650   **28 March**. Cromwell captures Kilkenny.
        10 April. Last Confederation forces in Munster are
        defeated.
        27 April. Montrose is defeated at Carbisdale in Scotland.
        21 May. Montrose is executed.
        21 June. The Ulster army is destroyed at Scariffhollis.
        3 September. Scots are defeated at Dunbar by Cromwell.
1651   **1 January**. Charles II is crowned in Scotland.
        July. Charles dodges past Cromwell and invades England.
        28 August. General Monck captures the Committee of
        Estates in Scotland.
        1 September. General Monck captures Dundee.
        3 September. Cromwell wins the battle of Worcester.
        16 October. Charles escapes to France.
        27 October. Limerick surrenders to Henry Ireton.
1652   **12 February**. Union offered to Scotland.
        21 April. Union of Scotland and the Commonwealth
        announced.
        12 August. Ireland: The Act of Settlement is put in place,
        moving Catholic landowners implicated in the war to
        lands west of the River Shannon.
1653   **4 March**. The Glencairn rebellion breaks out in the
        Scottish Highlands.
        20 April. Cromwell dissolves Parliament.
        29 April. A new Council of State is created.
        4 July. The Little Parliament or Barebones Parliament
        meets.
        12 December. Parliament dissolves itself.
        15 December. The Instrument of Government is
        accepted as the constitution of the Protectorate.
        16 December. Cromwell is appointed Lord Protector.

Principal places mentioned in the text.

Principal battles.

ONE

The Scottish Revolution

On Sunday 23 July 1637 an Edinburgh woman, Jenny
Geddes, is supposed to have thrown a folding chair
at the dean of St Giles Cathedral as he stood in the
pulpit. Whether or not Jenny herself was actually
involved, other women and men in the cathedral
certainly hurled their cutty stools at the dean and
launched the public and violent reaction to the
government of Charles I. This reaction ended
sixteen years later with the king executed, the
monarchy abolished and a united Britain of England,
Wales, Scotland and Ireland ruled as a republic from
Westminster. Of course the reasons why Jenny, or
whoever it was, first picked up a stool lay both in the
previous years of government and in discussions in
the tenements of Edinburgh's Royal Mile. There
were underlying structural causes too, economic and
religious as well as political, which dated from
around the time of the Protestant Reformations in
the four nations of the British Isles. However, these

1

long-term issues generated the very great stresses and strains apparent during Charles I's reign.

There were three principal problems with Charles's relationship with Scotland: government, property and religion. With regard to the first, the king had tried to govern Scotland as his father, James VI and I had done, with the pen from Westminster. To secure easy and obedient government, Charles attempted to pack the executive – the Scottish Council – with 'yes men': Scotsmen he had recently ennobled and favoured in the hope that as he had made them successful and they owed him everything, they would, in return, be loyal to him. Loyal they may have been, but as they were new men they had few contacts and only scanty political networks from which to draw advice and support. This could only weaken the effectiveness of government.

In terms of property, Charles exploited tradition in a way which angered the principal leaders of Scottish society. When a monarch was crowned he or she was given the right to rescind grants of land made during his or her minority years. The original idea was to prevent permanent alienations of property made by Scotland's many infant monarchs while under the influence of guardians or regents who might thereby have benefited. Charles, though, sought to regain all the grants of land he had made before and after he had reached his majority, up until his coronation. In part he intended to use some of this land – that which had formerly belonged to the monasteries dissolved in the Reformation – to fund the Scottish church.

This seemingly useful motive was open to hostile interpretation: Charles, like his father before him, favoured an episcopal structure for the state church, and therefore his Scottish subjects were suspicious. They were used to a Presbyterian system with a church hierarchy comprising elected leaders, rather than men appointed by the monarch, as in an episcopate. Charles's attempts to fund the church could be interpreted as an attempt to bolster the episcopal elements of the Kirk at the expense of the elected officials. The seizure of land by the king could also be interpreted as an attack on the property rights of the Scottish nobility and gentry – the lairds. Combined with fears about his religious policy, this did nothing to endear the king to his Scottish subjects.[1]

The third element, religion, was a problem in its own right. Charles's father had longed to convert the Reformation church in Scotland from a Presbyterian hierarchy to an episcopal system, with bishops and archbishops in charge of church government. His attempts to alter the church had met with mixed success, and by the time of his death James had accepted that compromise was necessary and so the Kirk retained elements of both systems. Charles would recognize no such compromise. At his Scottish coronation, delayed until 1633, he made it clear that the English church was to be regarded as the model for Kirk reform, with Church of England representatives taking precedence over Scottish officials, who were made to wear English style attire.[2] By the mid-1630s Charles had a team of Scottish bishops, with English advice, drafting a new prayerbook. This service book, intended to be similar to that used in England, was to lay down the annual pattern of worship and set out the form of Kirk service to be held in churches throughout the country. By 1637 the book was ready, and on 23 July 1637 the dean of St Giles mounted the pulpit steps to read the new service.

Before it was even opened, the service book was feared by many Scots men and women who saw it as the first step towards a return to the Roman Catholic faith. At the very least it could be seen as an unwanted Anglification of the Kirk. In the wake of the riot in the cathedral, similar events occurred elsewhere in Edinburgh and then throughout Scotland. People rioted in the streets and clergy who conformed to the king's wishes were attacked. The anger against the king's actions was felt at all levels of Scottish society; although members of the nobility did organize some of the riots, the participants were all too willing to take part and just as angry as the nobles. The king's response was to blame a radical minority, and he ordered the Council to deal with it. However, the Council was already weak because of Charles's interference with its composition: its members had little political ability and were unable to command the respect of the rioters. The Council was also not wholehearted in its support of the king. Many members had stayed away from St Giles because they knew what would happen, and now sections of the Council were talking with the king's opponents. Moreover, the councillors also began to petition the king, asking him to relax or even change his policies. There followed a period when a series of misunderstandings dogged Charles's dealings with the Council as they attempted to convince him that the service book was regarded as an intolerable innovation by the people, and he professed to believe that the people had been misled into thinking that it contained innovations that would lead to popery. All that was needed, he said, was for the message to be changed: the policy would not change.

Opponents outside the Council drafted a *Supplication and Complaint* which they presented to it on 18 October 1637. The supplicants blamed the bishops for all the trouble, and claimed that the prayerbook was unconstitutional and that it did a disservice to the English Book of Common Prayer upon which it was based, because it was essentially a corrupt version. The presentation of the *Supplication* was accompanied by enthusiastic demonstrations and riots.[3] Charles ordered that the leading supplicants be arrested. By the time his chief Scottish minister, the Earl of Traquair, journeyed to London to try to persuade him that the situation was serious and that imperious orders were not the answer, the earl's enemies had convinced the king that Traquair was doing deals with the supplicants. Charles refused even to consider the *Supplication* and instead took full responsibility for the prayerbook. Naturally, he expected that the supplicants, who had until now avoided blaming him directly, would cease their rebellion because they dared not attack the king personally. They did not take any notice. Instead Archibald Johnston of Wariston and Alexander Henderson drafted the National Covenant on behalf of the king's opponents. This reaffirmed the Negative Confession of 1581 whereby James VI and his people had sworn to defend the Protestant church. The Covenant also implied that religious changes approved by the General Assembly, the supreme body of the Kirk, since 1581, might have been unconstitutional: it was referring to all legislation relating to episcopacy.[4]

The Covenant was signed by nobles and lairds gathered at St Giles, Edinburgh, on 28 February 1638, and was sent first to other Edinburgh ministers, then to people in the town, and later throughout the whole country. As the people of Scotland signed it, the king's opponents in the capital formed an executive committee, known as the fifth table, to coordinate the work of the four committees established in December 1637 to represent the church, the nobles, the lairds and the burgesses of the towns who had come together as supplicants. The fifth table now negotiated directly with the king's representative, Traquair, and his successor the Marquis of Hamilton.[5] The latter was unable to slow down the impetus for change in Scotland, and eventually he and king agreed to call the General Assembly that the Covenanters demanded to ratify their actions. Hamilton tried to control the elections to the assembly and it was set to meet in Glasgow rather than in Edinburgh where Hamilton and Charles believed their principal opponents to be.

In addition, Hamilton inspired a new covenant, the King's Covenant, again based on the Negative Oath but with a bond of loyalty to the king added. This, it was hoped, would draw people away from the National Covenant, but instead many ignored it or simply signed it as well, not seeing any incompatibility between it and the National Covenant.[6] The General Assembly proved intractable and Hamilton could not influence its actions as it ratified the Covenant and disestablished the episcopacy and all the acts supporting it. Hamilton and the king now prepared for war, while continuing talks with the Covenanters. By the spring of 1639 the king's plans were well under way, and the Scots had begun to establish a military system based on county war committees. In March 1639 the Covenanters took control of Dunbarton, Aberdeen, where there had been opposition to the Covenant, and Edinburgh Castle. There were rumours that they intended to march on Carlisle and Berwick upon Tweed.

By May Charles had an army on the Scottish borders, and in June the Earl of Huntly seized Aberdeen for the king. This anti-Covenanter rebellion was crushed when the Earl of Montrose defeated Huntly at the Battle of the Bridge o' Dee on 19 June. Further south the war never really got started. On 4 June a party of the king's army under the Earl of Holland entered Scotland and near Kelso came across the Covenanter army led by Sir Alexander Leslie. Shots rang out and in the confusion that followed the English fled the field.[7] In the wake of this humiliating confrontation, peace negotiations began.

The Pacification of Berwick resulted in both armies being stood down, but it did not solve the problems that had brought the king and Scotland to war. Nor did the treaty end Charles's hostile ambitions. He still refused to accept the position of the Covenanters and, backed by growing confidence among his officers, he prepared once more for war. He had agreed to hold a meeting of the Estates later in the year, but also declared that a new General Assembly would meet, with bishops in attendance, and he hoped that this would annul the acts of the November 1638 session. The king was flying in the face of reality: there were now no bishops in Scotland and his actions caused riots in Edinburgh. Moreover, when it met in August 1638 the new General Assembly ratified all the acts of its predecessor.[8]

The meeting of the Estates was also well planned. The steering committee, the Lords of the Articles, normally controlled by the king's supporters, set about restructuring the Estates, downgrading their own role to ensure full debates on legislation when the Estates began to meet at the end of August. The result was that the Estates were dominated by the Covenanters and their programme. The king refused to ratify the Lords of the Articles' work and on 14 November he prorogued the Estates until 2 June 1640. So angry were the Covenanters that they appointed a committee to sit at Parliament House until the sessions reopened.

Meanwhile Charles planned again for war. He called parliaments in Ireland and in England (see chapters two and three) to provide him with money and ordered the mustering of his forces in northern England. The Irish Parliament ordered the collection of subsidies to pay for the war, but the Westminster Parliament did not. Even so, Charles planned to invade Scotland in the summer of 1640. Before he could do so the Covenanter army crossed the Tweed and on 28 August defeated the king's army at the battle of Newburn.[9] This time the Scots were able to impose terms at the negotiating table: their army, which occupied the north of England for the next year, was to be paid for by taxes raised in England, and the king was to end his attempts to interfere with the Kirk. The Scots also demanded that a Parliament at Westminster should ratify the treaty.

During the next year the work of the Scottish political revolution was confirmed. The roles of the monarch and the executive were reduced while the Estates' role in government increased. A Triennial Act ensured that the Estates would meet at least every three years regardless of whether or not the monarch willed it. While this radicalism drove some moderate Covenanters, including the Earl of Montrose, over to the king, Charles was now so powerless that in the summer of 1641, when he travelled to Edinburgh to ratify the Treaty of London, he was also obliged to ratify his diminution in the Scottish governmental process. The king had harboured hopes of forming an important body of supporters in Scotland that summer, but Montrose was imprisoned and the attempted *coup d'état* in October was betrayed and failed completely. Charles had hoped to have Hamilton, now a Covenanter himself, and his brother arrested. He expected this would destabilize the Covenanter leadership and allow him to re-establish government with his supporters.[10] Instead, after this ignominious defeat, Charles returned to England where the Scottish rebellion was being emulated.

TWO

The Irish Rebellion

Ireland was regarded as a nation belonging to the monarch of England by right of conquest: Henry VIII had incorporated Ireland as a kingdom and taken the crown himself. Since the twelfth century the English and their Norman predecessors had held land in Ireland, where they had established communities and regions governed in an English manner throughout the Middle Ages. This territory was in decline by the fifteenth century and English authority had diminished considerably by Henry VIII's reign. Initiatives by Henry and his daughter Elizabeth I had the effect of reinvigorating English and Welsh colonization, which in turn prompted the Gaelic Irish into rebellion. Defeat of these rebellions was followed by large-scale property confiscations which led to more land being available for colonists. The last province to undergo significant colonization was Ulster. Swathes of this province were colonized following the Nine Years War

(1594–1603) and the subsequent flight of the earls (Tyrconnell and Tyrone). During the war Tyrone had led the resistance to English rule, and although he had come to terms with James VI and I, he and his allies were steadily being isolated. Fears for their safety in these circumstances led to their flight, but James claimed that this was a treasonable act and the earls' lands were seized and opened for colonization.

The long process of interaction between the English (and Welsh) and the Irish had created a society with many layers by the 1630s. The majority of the people were Gaelic Irish and Roman Catholics. Their social and political leaders were generally in decline, although there were exceptions, such as the Earl of Clanricarde, who had demonstrated his loyalty to the crown, and the Earl of Ormond, who had assumed the Protestant faith. Outside Ireland there was a group of dispossessed Gaelic Irish, descendants of those who had lost land in the sixteenth and seventeenth centuries. Some of them had felt the impetus of the Roman Catholic counter-Reformation and saw their personal situation in terms of a war against the Protestant faith. The next group, in terms of length of time in Ireland, were the Old English (or, as they were sometimes called in Ireland, the New Irish). These were descendants of the families who had settled there in the Middle Ages. Most were Roman Catholic and many had adopted elements of Gaelic Irish culture. These families, once a part of England's rule in Ireland, were now being displaced by the next group: the New English. This group, which included prominent Welsh figures, consisted of those who had moved into Ireland during the later sixteenth and early seventeenth centuries; they were steadily taking up the reins of government as the Old English were excluded on the grounds of their religion. There was also one other group: the Scots. Attempts were made before 1603 to prevent Scottish settlement in Ulster, but there were already considerable relationships between the two countries, with clans from the Western Isles, such as the MacDonalds, having extensive family lands on both sides of the North Channel. From 1603 onwards Scottish settlement in Ulster was encouraged and Presbyterians fleeing James VI and I's and then Charles's assaults on the Kirk had settled there in the more liberal atmosphere of the Church of Ireland.

Charles's reign saw a determined effort to make the kingdom of Ireland a profitable possession. From 1633 the government of the nation was in the hands of Sir Thomas Wentworth, who enacted a governmental policy known as 'Thorough', with financial, political and religious aims.[1] In financial terms the king sought to gain money by forcing the Catholic Irish to surrender their land titles to him for a legally recognized re-grant, enforcing the law in prerogative courts in order to acquire the income generated by fines. He also took individual measures, such as fining the City of London for its failure to colonize the area around Derry (renamed Londonderry) in Ulster as planned. In political terms the king wanted Wentworth to control the Dublin Parliament through patronage and to have the Gaelic Irish and many of the Old English largely excluded from it. In religious terms the liberal regime of the Church of Ireland was to be tightened up. The Archbishop of Armagh, James Ussher, was pushed into the background and from 1634 John Bramhall, Bishop of Derry, took charge of running the church along similar lines to those of the Church of England under Archbishop William Laud.

The effect of these changes was, as C.V. Wedgwood noted, to unite the disparate groups in Ireland against Wentworth. There were some successes: the Parliament of 1634 was manipulated adroitly by Wentworth and his agents, and income did rise. Yet some plans, such as the opening of plantations in Connacht, failed and the redevelopment of the Catholic church continued apace. When the Scottish rebellion began in 1638, Wentworth was faced with the problem of the Presbyterians in Ulster signing the National Covenant (see chapter one). To combat this Wentworth declared that signing it was an act of treason. This prohibition was coupled with an oath of abjuration. Known together as the Black Acts, their effect was to drive many Scots from their homes in Ulster. As a result of their return to Scotland observers commented that large tracts of land were left untilled in the province. This, together with the suspension of the lucrative trade between Scotland and Ireland during the Anglo-Scottish war, with its concomitant loss of customs duties, exacerbated an economic downturn in Ireland.[2]

Wentworth's seemingly tight control made it obvious that Charles would try to exploit Ireland's resources to fight the war against Scotland. Wentworth was ordered to remodel the Irish army in preparation for an invasion of Scotland. But the king and Wentworth were not alone in wishing to use Ireland's resources against the Covenanters. The Earl of Antrim, head of the MacDonald or MacDonnell clan, was also prepared to exploit the situation. His people had been driven from most of their Western Scottish lands since the end of the fifteenth century by the Scottish monarchs and their agents, the Campbell clan. Antrim now proposed landing an army of MacDonalds on the west coast of Scotland. This would cost the king very little as the army would be in effect a clan force bound by loyalty to the clan chief and feudal dues. Wentworth was hostile to the proposal: on one level he doubted Antrim's acumen, but he also realized that this offer owed a great deal to Antrim's aim to regain much of his clan's lost lands.[3] The Campbells, notably Lord Lorne, later Marquis of Argyle, were prominent in the Covenanter leadership. Defeating the Covenanters would also result in the fall of the Campbells, with the MacDonalds ready to benefit from their enemy's fall. In the first war against Scotland Irish forces played little part, although a contingent helped to seize Carlisle. However, Wentworth's Ireland was to play a major role in Charles's attempts to finance the second war.

In March 1640 Wentworth convened a Parliament with the aim of providing funds for the war (and partly to encourage the English and Welsh Parliament due to meet in April to do the same) Again, Wentworth's power was more of an image than a reality, but his Parliament voted through four subsidies, each of £45,000, prefacing them with a statement declaring the Parliament's thanks for his wise government. However, as soon as the Lord Deputy left Ireland to help Charles with his preparations for the Westminster Parliament, this pliable unity began to break down. The subsidy rates were questioned and the enthusiastic tone of the preface queried. The English and Welsh Parliament was unimpressed by the four subsidies from Dublin and refused to discuss advancing money to the king (see chapter three) until he answered its grievances. The plans for war were pushed ahead regardless.

While Wentworth's back was turned the second session of the Dublin Parliament met on 1 June and downgraded the value of the second and subsequent subsidies from £45,000 to £9,922 10s 8d each.[4] Wentworth's government was questioned, especially with regard to the disenfranchisement of seven boroughs; his agent Sir Christopher Wandesworth was unable to control parliamentary business and prorogued Parliament on 17 June. When the Dublin Parliament met again on 1 October Charles had lost the war, Scotland was controlling the peace negotiations and the writs summoning a new Westminster Parliament had been sent out. Wentworth, now raised in the peerage to the Earl of Strafford, was under attack in all four nations as a fomentor of war.

Wandesworth tried to persuade the earl to prorogue Parliament again, but, alienated from the realities of Dublin by distance and ineffective communications, Strafford demanded that the Connacht plantations be discussed and approved before Parliament ended its session. This allowed time to develop opposition further, and Parliament drafted a remonstrance of sixteen legal, economic and political grievances about Strafford's rule to be presented to the king. Wandesworth, alerted to this, prorogued the session but not before a committee of representatives had been established to go to the king with the Remonstrance.[5]

This remonstrance provided a good deal of evidence for the trial of the Earl of Strafford (see chapter three) by the Westminster Parliament, which had ordered Strafford's arrest at the end of 1640. In Ireland Strafford's regime was dismantled; Wandesworth and George Radcliffe, another of Strafford's officials, were arrested and confidence in the attainability of reform began to grow. An alliance of Old and New English MPs drafted a set of 21 Queries which, although seemingly aimed at Strafford's government, actually questioned the very structure of government in the Irish kingdom. Although the executive Council attempted to delay dealing with the queries, the Commons debated them thoroughly in the July 1641 sessions in the wake of Strafford's execution.[6] The Catholic Irish, partly excluded from the Dublin parliamentary process, also harboured grievances, many of them related to the security of land ownership. These issues were focused on 'the Graces', a series of terms by which Charles, out of his grace and favour, was to recognize their tenure and tacitly tolerate their religion. After many delays, he indicated that he would ratify the Graces in 1641 but he was really powerless to do so. While the Scots were able to secure their church, and the English and Welsh were freed from Charles's religious reforms by the Long Parliament, the possibilities for recognizing the Roman Catholic faith in Ireland were limited. Moreover, the new Lord Lieutenant, the Earl of Leicester, had suggested that the regime in Ireland might be liberalized. Poyning's Law, which maintained that any proposed legislation in the Dublin Parliament had first to be approved in London, could be abolished.[7] The king disagreed. The majority population was then caught between two opposing forces – the hostility of both the Edinburgh and Westminster parliaments to toleration for Catholicism and the king's refusal to accept the diminution of his prerogative power in Ireland. Coupled with economic decline following the war, and fears that there was a determination to extirpate the Catholic faith, the situation became explosive.

A series of discussions held by Gaelic Irish landowners and some of the exiles during 1641 was aimed at overthrowing the weakened English regime. Other discussions took place between the Old English and the Gaelic Irish, and between the Gaelic Irish and the Roman Catholic church. The plot which emerged in October 1641 principally concerned the Gaelic Irish in Ulster and some of the exiles, notably Owen Roe O'Neill, a principal heir to the Earl of Tyrone.[8] On 22 October 1641 risings in Ulster ensured the capture of principal fortresses across the province, but attempts to seize Dublin that night came to nothing and the chief city was left in the hands of the English authorities. Within days the rebellion spread across Ireland. At first, some attempts were made to restrict the wrath of the rebels to English settlers who were dispossessed and sometimes herded towards ports so they could be transported to England. In a few places, the anger of those who feared that they and their religion were to be exterminated led to individual Protestants being murdered in rash acts of brutality, or in larger numbers where rioters were difficult to control. Reports of these murders quickly escalated into

21

myths of wholesale slaughter, which were put into print and carried to England, Wales and Scotland where they had an enormous effect on attitudes to the Irish people and the Irish war.

By the end of the year the Old English had joined the rebellion, and Sir Phelim O'Neill, commanding the rebels in Ulster, declared that the king had authorized the rising. In the early stages of the developing war, government forces under the Earl of Ormond scored successes against the rebel armies in Leinster and southern Ulster, but it soon became clear that the rebellion was on such a huge scale that the royal forces in the country were simply inadequate to deal with it. As the rebels began to structure their forces and resources nationwide, regiments from Scotland were landed in the north-east in May 1642, while money was being urgently raised in England and Wales to fund attempts to defeat the rebels. The effects of the rebellion began to spread across the Irish Sea and impinged directly on the disintegrating political situation in England and Wales.

THREE

The English and Welsh
Rebellion

There is great debate as to the condition of England
and Wales in the 1630s, and much of this centres on
the government of Charles I. Since 1629, when his
relations with Parliament were strained to breaking
point, the king had governed his southern and
eastern nations without the help of a Parliament.
Both England and Wales were at that time
represented by one body, based at Westminster. A
series of ineffective military interventions in
European affairs had resulted in questions about the
efficacy of Charles's policies, and the way in which tax
revenue was being spent. Questions had also been
asked about the king's religious beliefs, which
seemed to favour a shifting of the focus of the church
from its Calvinist teachings towards an Arminian
approach, feared by some as a step towards returning
England and Wales to the Roman Catholic church.

Some of these concerns surfaced as soon as Charles became king in 1625. Finance had been at the core of the disagreements between king and Parliament through the 1620s. In 1628 Parliament had become so concerned at Charles's taxation policies that it drafted the Petition of Right to guarantee property rights in the face of illegal taxation. The Petition had also reasserted the position of Parliament as the normal channel through which taxes should be raised. However, although Charles had assented to the Petition of Right, after repeated attacks on his religious aims he dissolved Parliament in 1629, thus ending any chance for MPs to further influence government policy. With Parliament out of the way, Charles continued to raise money in a manner that contravened the Petition of Right, for example, introducing fines for those who had not taken up a knighthood at his coronation and reintroducing fines for encroachments on royal forests, proven by resurrecting long-forgotten boundaries. He had also extended Ship Money, a coastal defence tax used to build and arm ships, to all inland counties in addition to the seaboard counties normally charged. Moreover, year after year from 1634 onwards, the king collected Ship Money as if it were an ordinary levy and not an extraordinary one to be collected in times of danger.

In religious issues, the king made no effort to allay the fears of those who had questioned his policies in the 1620s. He had steadily placed Arminians into bishoprics and college headships, and by 1633 had his principal agent William Laud consecrated as Archbishop of Canterbury. This enabled the speeding up of changes; the Liturgy and orders relating to vestments were strictly enforced and conformity in all ecclesiastical matters was controlled through reinvigorated church courts. Emphasis in church services was switched away from scripturally based sermons towards the ceremonial aspects of communion which was once again enacted as a sacrament. To some observers these changes, and the increased role of leading church officials in secular government, suggested that Charles was allying himself with the Catholic Counter-Reformation that was attempting to overthrow the Protestant faith in Europe.

The debate on the nature of England and Wales centres upon the reactions to Charles's government. The questions relate to the type of opposition, and whether it was significant and widespread, or of little importance. There was opposition to Ship Money, but it has been argued that this was on a small scale and in any case the king was able to build an impressive fleet. There was some opposition to

religious change but apart from a few very public
martyrs, such as the pamphleteers William Prynne,
John Bastwicke and Henry Burton, who were
pilloried and imprisoned for attacking reforms, and
those who emigrated to the Americas, there was
little trouble.[1] These arguments are not without
foundation, but they do not explain why the decade
came to an end with the king enmeshed in an
expensive war against Scotland.

In any case, these assertions can also be
challenged for the period before the war. Evidence
suggests that an increasing number of Ship Money
defaulters appeared before the courts. Arguments
that opposition remained low-key would be more
valid had not the trial of John Hampden, a Ship
Money defaulter, become a national *cause célèbre*. The
case went before the twelve judges of the king's
prerogative courts, and Hampden's lawyer, Oliver
St John, based his defence on the length of time
during which the tax had been collected. He did not
dispute the king's right to levy the tax in an
emergency, instead arguing that enough time had
now elapsed, since the first writs for collection, for a
Parliament to have been called and ordinary taxes to
have been collected. Five of the judges decided in
Hampden's favour. Although he lost the case, the
fact that five of the senior judges had disagreed with

the king was seen as a victory. Throughout the country opposition in the form of public protest and court appearances increased. This coincided with the escalation of the conflict with Scotland, and when Coat and Conduct levies were ordered to cover the military costs, a tax-payers' strike was engendered.

The war with Scotland was always going to cause problems for Charles and his government in England and Wales. This international aspect of his rule is the key to understanding why the king's reign fell apart in the way that it did. He was probably trying to rule his four nations as if they were one, and although the people in those four countries were not homogenous, many of them were united by a shared resentment at being regarded by Charles's government as a single problem. In each of the four nations Charles's centralizing policies were rejected, at least partly in Scotland and Ireland because the policies had a distinct English focus; this may also have been true of some elements within Wales. The social, religious and political issues merged in all four nations, with attacks on property being related to taxation, and taxation being related to war, and war being related to the religious impositions that were part of Charles's one-nation politics of order and conformity.

Thus, when Charles sought to go to war with the Scots because they rejected his religious policy, his English and Welsh subjects were querulous. The reforms initiated by Laud and Charles in England and Wales had affected everyone: the form of worship, the layout of the churches had been altered and some people were no doubt reminded of Roman Catholic forms of service and church layout, even if proportionately few emigrated or set up or joined secret conventicles. Called upon to fund and fight a war to impose upon the Kirk similar changes to those they disliked or distrusted at home, many English and Welsh people objected. Tax collection slowed down and the Trained Bands, the county-based militia, behaved in a riotous manner when in 1639 they were assembled to fight the Scots.[2]

The Pacification of Berwick in June 1639, coming so soon after the assembling of the English forces, ended the bad behaviour of the Trained Bands which were quickly dispersed. The king's preparations for resuming the war a year later raised hopes of change but just as quickly dashed them. The news that there was to be a Parliament in the spring of 1640 initiated a flood of petitions to Westminster objecting to the king's government. When Parliament assembled on 13 April 1640 the king expected it to follow the example of the March

Dublin Parliament and finance his military effort, while the electorate and others expected it not only to end the heavy burden of Ship Money and Coat and Conduct Money but also to confront the king about his religious policies. Yet both sides were to be frustrated. John Pym, an experienced parliamentarian, encapsulated the people's grievances under three headings: the king's treatment of his opponents in the 1629 Parliament (one had died in prison and another still languished in the Tower); the infringement of property rights enshrined in the Petition of Right; and religion.[3] Until these issues were dealt with, the House of Commons would not discuss new taxation. The king wanted the reverse: vote for taxes and then discuss grievances. By now the king's stock was so low with Parliament that he was not trusted, and it was felt that a quick vote for taxes might well have been followed by the closure of Parliament. In the end, after some three weeks, Charles dissolved Parliament anyway and embarked on his war on the cheap. He dredged up medieval commissions of array and created county committees to raise and provide funding for troops until they crossed the county boundary. Even so, the commissioners had trouble getting in sufficient funds – although this turned out to be the least of the troubles with the Trained Bands. As the soldiers moved northwards sections mutinied and went on the rampage, killing tame deer in a Leicestershire park, breaking into gaols and releasing prisoners in Derby. Everywhere soldiers broke into churches and destroyed the furniture introduced by Laud: altars and altar rails were particular targets. In some places mutinous soldiers even murdered their officers. When the army reached the northern border, military preparations proceeded apace, but not quickly enough to prevent a rapid march by the Scottish Army of the Covenant which crossed the Tweed and on 28 August 1640 defeated the king's army at Newburn.[4] Withdrawal became a full-scale retreat and the Scots occupied northern England, and forced the king to accede to their peace terms.

An important part of the peace terms was that any treaty had to be ratified by a Westminster Parliament. Demands for a Parliament had been made in England and Wales ever since the expulsion of what was known as the Short Parliament of April and May, and on the day that the Scots defeated the royal army twelve peers submitted a petition to the king calling for a Parliament.[5] The king had tried to summon a Grand Council of peers (a House of Lords in all but name) in the hope that they would prove more tractable than the Commons – he may have felt that back in April he had made some headway in the Lords. However, the demand for a Parliament was too strong, and after Newburn there was no chance of peace without one. Writs were sent out for a November session and the king tried his best to manipulate the elections. His efforts came to very little and the Parliament that met in November was overwhelmingly opposed to his government. Six months later Charles could count on the support of only around 10 per cent of the MPs.

Straight away, as the Scots Commissioners and parliamentary representatives began work on the Treaty of London, Parliament began to deconstruct the government. With Irish and Scottish cooperation, the Earl of Strafford was impeached, as was Laud; both were imprisoned in the Tower. Two other ministers were also in danger. Lord Finch, who as Speaker of the Commons in 1629, was felt to have cooperated with the king in dissolving Parliament, and Francis Windebanke, a minister thought to have favoured Catholics while persecuting godly puritans, fled into exile before they were impeached.[6]

The next six months saw the destruction of the machinery of Charles's government. The Court of High Commission which had presided over Archbishop Laud's reforms was abolished. Unpopular legislation such as that dealing with Ship Money was swept away. New legislation was enacted to ensure that Parliament played a permanent role in government. The Triennial Act was modelled on the Scottish act and ensured that a Parliament would meet at least every three years, while a dissolution act ensured that the present Parliament could only be dissolved with its own consent. In May Strafford was executed by an Act of Attainder which was passed after his elaborate trial at Westminster came unravelled for lack of evidence.[7] In June 1641 the king was presented with Ten Propositions which outlined a greater role for Parliament in choosing ministers and in foreign policy. Only religious reform had faltered, for while Parliament was agreed on what it did not want, like the Laudian policies, it was not united on wide-scale reforms aimed at removing bishops from the church.

Nevertheless, the king was powerless. With no great political support in Parliament he had become involved in the Army plot in the spring of 1641, which was aimed at rescuing Strafford from the Tower and imposing military force on Parliament. The plot had been exposed, resulting in Strafford's death and imperilling the queen who had also been involved. In the summer of 1641 Charles journeyed to Scotland to ratify the Treaty of London (see chapter one) and to acknowledge officially the reduction in his power north of the border by assenting to the reforming acts. There his plans to undertake a *coup d'état* failed and he became further isolated.

On Charles's return to London in November 1641, news of the rebellion in Ireland (see chapter two) reached England. Immediately plans for raising troops to send over the Irish Sea dominated parliamentary business. At the same time John Pym and his allies presented the Commons with the *Grand Remonstrance* which both set out Parliament's role in redressing the problems that had beset the country in the previous twelve years and demanded a greater role in executive government, including foreign policy. The Commons' debate on the *Remonstrance* dragged on into the early hours of 23 November, splitting the house like nothing else since the previous year, and its passing and publication drove some MPs to the king's side.[8] Strengthened by this sudden surge in support, Charles, while continuing to negotiate with Parliament, began to try to gain military control of the City of London and Westminster, placing Sir Thomas Lunsford in command at the Tower. This provoked public anger, just as many young London apprentices and their masters began to demand the expulsion of the bishops from the House of Lords.

Christmastide 1641 saw mob riots in the city and in neighbouring Westminster, Parliament was invaded, Westminster Abbey was stormed by a mob and the gates of Whitehall were attacked on the last day of the year.[9] The king made one more effort on 5 January. Escorted by an armed guard, he marched into Westminster and, leaving the guard outside the door, entered the Commons. There he demanded that five MPs he had charged with treason the previous day be handed over, along with one member of the Lords, Lord Mandeville. However, the men had all been sneaked out of Westminster at the last moment and Parliament refused to cooperate. The king, humiliated, was forced to withdraw. Over the next few days members of the royal family were barracked in the streets and on 10 January 1642 the royal household left the city. Six weeks later Queen Henrietta Maria was sent to Europe to pawn the crown jewels for arms, while the king went north in search of support. The government of England and Wales was out of step, and Parliament redesigned itself to fill the gap just as the Edinburgh Estates had done some three years earlier.

FOUR

War in the Four Nations

In the early months of 1642 the war in Ireland
lost some of its impetus. The rebel forces had penned
the English garrisons into pockets around Cork,
Dublin, Enniskillen, Derry and Belfast. The town of
Drogheda was under siege and other areas were under
pressure, but the advance of the rebellion had been
halted. The situation changed dramatically from
March 1642 when 3,000 English and Welsh soldiers
arrived in Leinster; 10,000 Scottish soldiers arrived in
Ulster in early May. The Marquis of Ormond,
appointed to command the English forces in Leinster,
was now able to goon the offensive and relieve
Drogheda. He followed this victory by striking
into Leinster and retaking principal fortresses and
defeating the rebel army at Kilrush. In the north-east
a Scottish army under Robert Munro drove into
the heart of Ulster, defeated Sir Phelim O'Neill
at Kilwarlin Wood and recaptured Newry. There
was now a distinct possibility that the war in Ireland

could be won, and in England and Wales this possibility was exploited to the full in order to finance the military expedition.[1]

One of the final agreements between the king and the Westminster Parliament related to the funding of the war in Ireland. On 15 February the act creating the army dispatched in March was passed and a financial plan to support it enacted. A system of loans established in January had failed to create a large pool of funds and speculators were now asked to invest in the war by buying a share in 2,500,000 acres of land which would be confiscated from the rebels when the war was won. A nationwide tax was also instituted to raise £400,000 to pay for the English, Welsh and Scottish forces in Ireland. Ironically, it was the question of armed forces in Ireland that drove the final wedge between Charles and Westminster. The king hinted that he might raise an army and lead it in person to Ireland. Parliament was suspicious of his motives, suspecting that he might use such an army to suppress his opponents at home rather than the rebels in Ireland. The rebels had already claimed that they were acting in the king's name against 'Puritans', a label given to the king's opponents in England, Wales and Scotland as well as in Ireland.[2]

There followed protracted negotiations over Parliament's proposed Militia Bill which removed control of the Trained Bands from the king, and in the end Parliament took executive power and renamed the bill an ordinance, thus circumventing the need for the king's approval. With this ordinance Parliament took control of the militia, appointing the Lord Lieutenants who were the county commanders. In late May the king created committees or commissions in English and Welsh shires to command the Trained Bands and during the summer both sides postured and drilled their armed supporters, to little effect other than frightening the people and providing good copy for the burgeoning newspaper industry.

Towards the end of the summer both sides began to make more effective attempts to raise armies by giving commissions to wealthy active supporters who raised regiments in their home areas and led them to general musters.[3] Both sides had also made attempts to seize weapons and ammunition: as early as April the king had tried to gain control of the magazine deposited at Hull during the war with Scotland, but in the summer he diverted his efforts towards the magazines held in each of the midland counties of Nottinghamshire, Leicestershire and Warwickshire. By the time he tried to seize the Warwickshire magazine both sides had raised sufficient forces for fighting to break out on a significant scale, and the scuffles around Coventry and Warwick grew into civil war.

On 22 August the fighting was given official status when Charles raised his royal banner in the precincts of Nottingham Castle. Within a month he was assembling an army in the vicinity of Shropshire, drawing on Welsh and north-western support, while Parliament's commander, the Earl of Essex, assembled his forces in Northamptonshire. After victory in a skirmish on the outskirts of Worcester, the royalist army marched on London. Essex attempted to intervene, but was by-passed and had to chase the king forces until he caught them at Edgehill in Warwickshire. The battle on 23 October 1642 was inconclusive, but the defeat of hopes that one decisive battle would end years of political and military wrangling forced a change in the aspect of the war. Both sides now began to concentrate on the capture of territory and resources. Over the winter battles and skirmishes were fought across the country as both sides took possession of castles and towns, billeted soldiers on the surrounding communities and then instituted taxation systems to fund the war. The king's advance on London was halted at Turnham Green on 13 November after he had barged through Brentford the previous day.

In Ireland the promise of victory was snatched away from Monro and Ormond. Over the Irish Sea civil war absorbed the paymasters at Westminster. The king took charge of most of the £400,000 being raised in Wales and the north and west of England which had been allocated for the war in Ireland. Support for the war against the rebels dried up. At the same time, inspired by the Catholic clergy, the rebels reorganized themselves. As early as April 1642 Ulster clergy meeting at Kells in Armagh had organized the finances of Ulster's war effort. They had also declared that all the risings in the country were part of one rebellion and arranged a national synod in May which confirmed these assertions. Leinster followed suit and by June an Oath of Association was in place. A system of national government was proposed, with county and provincial assemblies working with a General Assembly based at Kilkenny. The armed forces were officially organized into four provincial armies. By October this was all in place and peace terms were proposed to Ormond. The king was asked to confirm the centrality of the Catholic church and the political representation of the Catholic people of Ireland. This new structure, combined with the decline in the ability of the British forces to pursue the war, put the Confederation of Kilkenny in the dominant position in Ireland. Its army was in control of all the country except for some pockets in east Ulster, around Dublin, and the Cork and Youghal area of Munster.

By the summer of 1643 the royalist forces were dominant in all of Wales except for Pembrokeshire while in England they controlled the north-east, the south-west and much of the midlands, leaving Parliament defending the south-east, the Thames Valley, Lancashire and Cheshire, some strategically important ports on the south coast and Hull on the east coast. In the autumn the royalists attempted to take these important targets: the Earl of Newcastle attacked Hull, Prince Maurice surrounded Plymouth and the king attacked Gloucester.

As royalist energies were consumed in these sieges, diplomacy and politics changed the face of the war. In Ireland, Ormond and the Confederation agreed a cease-fire, known as the Cessation. While this did not acknowledge the Confederation's demands, it secured the end of fighting and allowed Ormond to begin shipping home the English and Welsh forces sent there in 1642. All these forces were initially sent to fight for the king. At the same time as Ormond was negotiating in Ireland, the Scots had been discussing the war with the king and with Westminster. The royalists rejected the Scots' approaches and their offer to mediate, but John Pym and Parliament worked hard to make common cause with the Scots. Religion and mistrust of the king provided the dual keys. Pym argued that the king could not be trusted to stick to agreements made with the Estates or with the General Assembly. Moreover, Pym told the Scots that their king was rumoured to be negotiating with the Catholic Confederation. Pym even offered a restructuring of the church in England along similar lines to the Kirk in return for support.

When news of the Cessation arrived, any doubts about the treaty were swept away by the revelation that the king had negotiated with Catholics and that he had secured military aid from Ireland. While the Cessation did not, as yet, involve Catholic Irish troops being sent to Britain it might well happen in the future. The Estates and Parliament joined forces and signed the Solemn League and Covenant, binding them together in the name of God (and a Presbyterian church). A Council of Divines at Westminster would discuss the nature of the church in England and Wales, while a Scottish army – the Army of the Solemn League and Covenant – paid for by taxes raised in England and Wales, would enter England in January.[4]

The three royalist attacks on the garrisons had all failed. Newcastle's army wasted away outside Hull,

Plymouth was still in safe parliamentarian hands, and the Earl of Essex had marched from London to relieve Gloucester, and then defeated the king's army at Newbury on 20 September when Charles tried to prevent the earl from returning to London. The influx of English troops returning from Ireland because of the Cessation promised to change this situation. Those who arrived in Bristol were added to the western forces and the Oxford-based royalist army, while those who landed at Chester and along the North Wales coast were forged into a new large army with the potential to take control of the north-west of England and the Welsh border. Yet this force was defeated at Nantwich on 25 January and dispersed. Many of the soldiers had been reluctant royalists and now joined the parliamentarian forces. Meanwhile, the Army of the Solemn League and Covenant pushed down the east coast of England, tying up the Marquis of Newcastle's army and allowing the Yorkshire royalist forces under Lord Fairfax to take over parts of the marquis's territory. After the Battle of Selby on 11 April the Northern Army had to abandon attempts to hold back the Scots, and instead became trapped in York.

Three armies now converged on the northern royalists: the Scots, Fairfax's forces, and the Eastern Association army under the Earl of Manchester. The latter had marched from its East Anglian bases, having first restored parliamentarian fortunes in Lincolnshire which had suffered a blow when Prince Rupert and Lord Loughborough had defeated an army besieging the royalist garrison at Newark.[5]

The net tightened around York during June 1644, but already Prince Rupert had assembled an army and was marching through Lancashire to come to the rescue. In the midlands the king was playing cat and mouse with the Earl of Essex and Sir William Waller, who had attempted to close in on his capital in Oxford. The two parliamentarians were bitter rivals and as soon as the king broke out of Oxford, Essex set off with his own forces to march into the west. Waller chased the king around the midlands until at Cropredy Bridge in Oxfordshire the king turned on him and defeated his army. With Waller defeated, Charles turned and pursued Essex into the west. In the north Rupert had broken through and relieved York on 1 July only to be defeated the following day at Marston Moor by the three armies of Leven, Manchester and Fairfax.

This defeat saw the destruction not only of the prince's army but also of Newcastle's, and while Rupert was able to gather a cavalry force and escape across the Pennines, Newcastle, with no army left and his vast fortune spent, went into voluntary exile on the continent. The battle of Marston Moor had far-reaching consequences for the vast resources and man-power of the north of England were now lost to the king. These consequences were not immediately obvious, and although many of the king's supporters, including Lord Wilmot, the leader of his cavalry, thought that a negotiated peace should be aimed at, the king further boosted his confidence by defeating Essex at the battle of Lostwithiel in Cornwall on 1–3 September.[6]

Parliament now tried to reconstruct its forces by bringing Manchester's army southwards to join the remains of Essex's army and Waller's new army, and this new force was sent to capture Oxford's outpost garrisons. At Newbury on 27 October the parliamentarians were presented with an opportunity to defeat the outnumbered royalist army near Donnington Castle. But it was an opportunity lost as the coordination between the three armies broke down, allowing the king to escape. In the wake of this humiliation the parliamentarian side was wracked by division, as Manchester attacked his second-in-command, Oliver Cromwell, accusing him of religious subversion. Cromwell in turn accused Manchester of being unwilling to defeat the king.

This brought to the fore the division in Parliament between those who sought to defeat the king before discussing terms with him (the War Party) and those who wanted a negotiated settlement (the Peace Party). In addition to these issues there was also a religious problem: although a majority of the House of Commons wanted some form of Presbyterianism to be introduced into England and Wales, a significant number of MPs, backed by many army officers, wanted to have no state church, but rather a collection of equal congregations. This was the essence of Manchester's attack on Cromwell's religious position: Manchester was a Presbyterian, Cromwell an Independent. The Scottish alliance was a further complication: some elements of both the War Party and the Peace Party now wanted to end the Scots' involvement because since Marston Moor the Northern Army was felt to have contributed little to the war. Moreover, all Independents resented the Scottish influence on the Westminster Council of Divines which was moving towards establishing a Presbyterian church in England and Wales. The Scots mistrusted English Presbyterians whom they saw as 'soft', but they hated Cromwell, whom they thought had claimed the glory due to their commander David Leslie after Marston Moor, and his Independent friends.

Out of these angry exchanges came two resolutions: first, a new army had to be created and second, the army leaders could have no place in the legislative – a leader could not be both an MP and an officer, one or other had to be given up. The latter was unpopular and never fulfilled: it was unpopular with the House of Lords as it automatically disqualified all its members from command as they could not give up their place in the Lords, and it never operated fully because some MPs, including Sir William Brereton, a commander in the north-west, and Oliver Cromwell, were given dispensation to hold commands. The New Model Army which came into existence in early 1645 was really a formalized amalgamation of the armies humiliated at Newbury in 1644 made up to strength with conscripts, but its commanders were successful men and the logistical structure was initially sound. The commander of the New Model Army was Sir Thomas Fairfax, son of Lord Fairfax; his second-in-command was Oliver Cromwell from Manchester's army, and the Major-General of the Foot was Sir Philip Skippon from Essex's army.[7]

The year 1644 had seen major developments in Scotland when a force of Irish and Highland Catholic soldiers, mainly drawn from the MacDonnells and MacDonalds under Alasdair MacColla, landed in the Western Isles in the middle of the year. The Cessation had not ended the fighting in Ireland, for as soon as the Solemn League and Covenant had been signed, the Scottish forces in Ireland received a new impetus for fighting the Confederation. An important reason for sending MacColla to Ireland was the hope that a war in Scotland would induce the Scots to withdraw their forces from Ireland. By the end of the summer MacColla had been joined by the Marquis of Montrose who had few men but held a commission from the king as Lieutenant-General in Scotland. Montrose intended to foment a war that would initially force the Scots to withdraw their army from England, hoping perhaps that victory would result in a change of government in Edinburgh. In September Montrose defeated a Covenanter army at Tippemuir and then captured Aberdeen.

The winter of 1644/5 was spent in raiding and disrupting the peace of the Highland region as MacColla's MacDonalds took revenge on the Campbells of the Earl of Argyle on what had once been MacDonald lands. On 2 February 1645 Montrose's army defeated the Earl of Argyle at Inverlochy and embarked on a series of battles in which they defeated every army sent against it by Edinburgh. At Auldearn in the north-east, Montrose defeated John Hurry on 9 May. On 2 July he was in the eastern fringes of the Highlands where he defeated William Baillie at the Bridge of Alford. A march on Glasgow followed, and on 15 August Montrose defeated the last home army at Kilsyth. Scotland was now in his hands and the government tottered as he called a new session of the Estates to meet at Edinburgh (see chapter five).[8]

In England the king moved out of Oxford in early May 1645 to try to relieve the siege of Chester. In an effort to break the impasse in the Irish negotiations, Charles sent over a new negotiator, the Earl of Glamorgan, to conduct secret discussions with the Confederation, hoping that Irish troops would soon land at Chester. However, as he marched north-wards, the siege was abandoned and Charles turned eastwards, capturing Leicester at the very end of May. The loss of Leicester galvanized Parliament into action: Fairfax and the New Model Army were ordered to abandon the siege of Oxford, which they had begun after the king had left for Chester, to go north and attack the king. On 14 June they defeated the king at Naseby. Charles lost his most experienced army as well as a cabinet of letters that proved he was negotiating with the Catholic Irish. The New Model Army quickly turned south-west and defeated Lord Goring at Langport and then went on to seize important royalist strongholds throughout the region.

The king tried to create a new army in the

midlands and in South Wales, and on two occasions he was tempted to try to reach Montrose in Scotland, but failed to follow through the idea. The royalist army he had reassembled after Naseby was defeated in September outside Chester as he once again attempted to free the region for the landing of Irish troops. This defeat was quickly followed by the refusal of South Wales to raise any more troops, the surrender to the parliamentarians of Bristol, the other possible port for landing Irish troops, and the news of Montrose's defeat in Scotland. The royalist cause was defeated in England and Wales, even if the king did not realize it yet.

FIVE

War in Scotland

The campaigns of the Marquis of Montrose saw the
defeat of all the home armies in Scotland by mid-
August 1645. The battle of Kilsyth near Glasgow on
15 August seemed to have sealed the fate of the
Covenanter government. There had been a marked
reluctance among many royalists to join Montrose's
cause, partly because they feared the Covenanter
government at Edinburgh but also because they
were unhappy at the presence of the Irish troops
under MacColla and the Highland soldiers raised by
Montrose and MacColla in the west of Scotland. As
both these groups were essentially Roman Catholic,
the re-establishment of a Catholic church tended to
follow in the wake of the royalist Highland
conquests. There was also a dislike of Montrose
himself, who had been a leading Covenanter until
his change of heart in 1640/1. Indeed, the Gordon
clan of the Marquis of Huntly had been defeated by
Montrose when they tried to hold Aberdeen for the

king in the first Bishops' War (see chapter one), and Huntly in particular was loath to join the turn-coat's forces.

The victories Montrose had won did attract hesitant support from some of the waverers, but Kilsyth turned the tide and Montrose was met by many hitherto secret royalists, and a good many liars. The summoning of the Estates to Edinburgh offered Montrose the opportunity to establish a new government in Scotland, one which would withdraw troops from England, and perhaps Ireland too. As Montrose rested at Bothwell Castle and received his new-found supporters, MacColla returned to the Highlands to prevent a Covenanter force gathering in Ayrshire and then began a recruitment campaign in Argyll.[1]

There was irony in what happened next: part of the Army of the Solemn League and Covenant was withdrawn from England. It had been campaigning in the south-west midlands, attempting to drive a wedge between the royalists in England and Wales. David Leslie and 6,000 men left Lord Leven and marched rapidly through England and into Lowland Scotland. On 13 September Leslie reached Philliphaugh, where the bulk of Montrose's reduced forces were camped, and attacked them. The bloody battle which followed ended in the destruction of

Montrose's army and, after a year's hard campaigning, put an end to hopes of a royalist Scotland. Montrose himself escaped, but his men were slaughtered both on the field and afterwards in fits of Covenanter vengeance.

MacColla remained in the Highlands, where he was tackling the garrisons re-established by the Campbells. MacColla began systematically to exterminate the male Campbells of military age and destroyed Campbell property and supplies to hamper Covenanter military efforts in the region. It was the start of twenty months of vicious guerrilla warfare. In April 1646 MacColla was joined by the Earl of Antrim, his clan chief, and by reinforcements from Ireland. However, the next month the king, who had surrendered at Newark, ordered his supporters in the four nations to lay down their arms. The Marquis of Huntly and Montrose gave up the fight, but the MacDonnells/MacDonalds under their clan leaders, Antrim and MacColla, did not; their agenda had always been a double one, the war on the king's behalf long providing a convenient cover for regaining MacDonald lands lost to the Campbells.[2]

The Army of the Solemn League and Covenant had been instrumental in ending the war in England. In the wake of Naseby the king had never amassed an army sufficient to dent Parliament's growing hold on England and Wales. The royalist cause began to implode as the gentry of South Wales effectively threw the royalists out of the region in September and those of mid-Wales followed suit. The king and his forces failed to march north to join Montrose, and their last victory came when they forced the Scots to abandon their siege of Hereford. When the king did dispatch a party of horse towards Scotland, Montrose was already defeated and the party was attacked and chased through the north of England before finally being defeated at Carlisle. With the collapse of the secret treaty negotiated in Ireland by the Earl of Glamorgan (see chapter six), the king's eyes turned from Ireland as a place of possible salvation back to Scotland.

From the end of 1645 the Army of the Solemn League and Covenant had been working with the English Northern Association Army under Sydenham Pointz. Together these forces had surrounded Newark, a strategically important and large royalist garrison on the eastern border of Nottinghamshire. The king, aware that his opponents, the Scots and Parliament, were beginning to drift apart, hoped to drive a wedge between them. After the defeat of his last hastily gathered field army at Stow-on-the-Wold in March 1646, Charles left Oxford in disguise and rode to Newark where he surrendered to the Scots. He hoped that he could either win them over to his side by diplomacy where a military campaign had failed, or at least destroy the alliance between them and Parliament which would leave him in an advantageous position.[3] The Scots took the king away northwards with them, having forced him to order all his garrisons, starting with Newark, to surrender. A wedge was driven between the king's opponents, but this was not to lead to an open breach at first. The Scots insisted that negotiations be conducted with all parties involved, and when Parliament presented Charles with the *Newcastle Propositions* the Scots urged him to come to terms. The Scots on the other hand were not fully enamoured with the *Propositions* which left the church in England and Wales subject to parliamentary interference. They suspected that the English Presbyterians lacked spiritual fortitude, and they were particularly concerned about the appearance of radical Independent sects and congregations in England, which Parliament seemed unable or worse, unwilling, to control.

Charles rejected the *Newcastle Propositions*, claiming that the terms which changed the form of the church in England and Wales were against his conscience, that the loss of his military powers emasculated the monarchy, and that he could not abandon his friends (royalist military and civil commanders) to the justice of Parliament. By the end of January 1647, the Army of the Solemn League and Covenant had marched out of England, abandoning the king at Newcastle, in return for a much-reduced lump sum of back pay.

Their return from England freed Scottish soldiers for the war at home. David Leslie's forces marched first up the east coast to deal with the last vestiges of the Gordon's rebellion. By March all the Marquis of Huntly's garrisons had surrendered, and Leslie turned towards the Highlands. In the west of Scotland MacColla's forces had held tightly to their gains secured after Philliphaugh. Although a number of garrisons had fallen to the Earl of Argyle's Campbell forces, few efforts were made to meet MacColla in the field. One attempt to do so in 1646 had ended in disaster at Lagganmore and the defeat had led to the burning to death of captive men and women at *Sabhal nan Cnamh* (the 'Barn of Bones'). As Leslie approached, MacColla began to devastate the area through which he would pass: Inveraray was burned, Kilmartin, Kilmichael and Kilberry were destroyed. But Leslie marched on, through Dunblane, on to Dunaverty Castle whose garrison he massacred after they had surrendered.

Leslie's army reached the coast and then continued to pursue MacColla through the Isles. MacColla fled to Ireland, where he again took up arms; in his wake Leslie captured the last of the MacDonnell/MacDonald Irish-royalist garrisons, including Dunyveg, which was held by MacColla's father, Coll Ciotach, whom Argyle had hanged. Peace by the summer of 1647 brought an end to the 'official' fighting, but the Campbells continued to mark out their renewed hold on the Kintyre region. In an area devastated by war and plague there was little for them to do in many places but move new settlers on to empty lands.

Events in England soon spurred the Edinburgh government into reopening discussions with the king. First, the growth of radical political parties advocating a wider democracy and religious toleration seemed to be influencing the New Model Army leadership. Second, the army and Parliament were divided, arguing over issues such as the shape of the political settlement to end the war, the religious settlement, the arrears of pay owed to the New Model Army, and the attempt to raise a new army to send to Ireland. In July 1647 the army leaders, Fairfax, Cromwell and Ireton, approached Charles, who had been abducted from his parliamentary guards and taken into the army's keeping, offering him a new treaty of their own, the *Heads of the Proposals*. This worried the Scots (see chapter seven) as the *Heads* offered no religious guarantees for Scotland and had been drawn up by Independents. The king said that he approved the new treaty but this remark was for Scottish consumption only; he regarded the new treaty as essentially similar to the *Newcastle Propositions* and would eventually reject it. However, the effect on the Scots was electric. A number of approaches were quickly made to the king, trying to persuade him to make separate terms with Scotland.[4] By this time the army dominated Parliament and the city (see chapter seven) and was in a position of power. Some elements within the army were also discussing radical solutions to political problems in England and Wales with the radical group known as the Levellers.[5]

The king was now at Hampton Court, having been lodged there when the army marched on London and three Scottish Commissioners attempted to persuade the king to escape captivity during the autumn months. Again Charles played for time, hinting that he might flee north to the border, but delaying on the issue of whether he would sign the Covenant. Eventually, as the army and the Levellers met at Putney, Charles escaped, but went south,

ending up at Carisbrooke Castle on the Isle of
Wight, probably hoping to be allowed to slip away to
France. Charles had sent proposals for peace to
Parliament, but this move was not a genuine attempt
to conclude a treaty, as they really appealed to the
now powerless Presbyterian group. None the less
Parliament sent counter-proposals, the Four Bills, to
the king who, again for Scottish ears, initially said
that he liked them. The Scottish commissioners,
who had trailed after Parliament's representatives,
may have panicked: they hastily agreed terms with
the king, which would create a single political nation
of England, Wales and Scotland, with free trade, a
joint executive for important affairs of state and bi-
national representation on the Westminster and the
Edinburgh privy Councils. However, the king was
not committed to signing the Covenant. In return
for this apparent settling of Scottish affairs, the Scots
would send an army into England to restore the king
to power, so that the necessary legislation could be
pushed through the Westminster Parliament.

This agreement, the Engagement, was not really a
success for the Scots: it split the political leadership
at home and made the raising of an army difficult,
as many experienced Covenanter officers, freed for
duty by the ending of the Highland war, refused to
serve a non-Covenanter king. The hard-line

Covenanters were, however, in something of a minority as since the disappointments of 1646, the Marquis of Hamilton had been able to forge a more moderate faction in the government. This faction impressed upon the Estates its concerns over English backsliding on the nature of the church in England and Wales, and the need for guarantees for the future security of the Kirk. The Kirk was not convinced and the lies told by the Commissioners about Charles's attitude to the Covenant – they painted a more positive picture of his willingness to abide by it – were soon exposed, but little political opposition to the Engagement could be mounted.[6] The spring of 1648 was spent in preparing a new Scottish force: the Engager Army.

There was an attempt to make this into a pan-national venture to restore the king. Rebellions and risings were planned in England and Wales, building on disquiet about parliamentary government and continued taxation which had already inspired risings in London, Canterbury and Norwich. The Marquis of Ormond, who had left Ireland in 1647, was to return to forge an alliance between royalists and the Confederation of Kilkenny (see chapter six) with the hope of securing victory in Ireland against the English and Welsh parliamentarian forces there, and then bringing forces across the Irish Sea to aid the king. (The Scots would, it was hoped, abide by the Engagement.) Plans were also made for bringing Scots forces from Ulster to join the Engager Army's invasion of England. The stage was set for renewed war in Britain, and it began, rather unexpectedly, in Wales.

SIX

War in Ireland

Cessation had not ended the war in Ireland. There were still 'border disputes' on the fringes of the English 'pockets' in Leinster, Munster and Connacht. In Ulster there was full-scale war as Confederation forces under Owen Roe O'Neill tried to wrest control from Robert Monro's Scots. Nevertheless, apart from Antrim and Down, which were in Scots hands, and the small English pockets, the Confederation held sway throughout Ireland in the months after the Cessation. It had felt able to dispatch troops to Scotland (see chapter four), although this meant drawing Scottish troops from Ulster.

The decline in the king's fortunes in England and Wales had several effects on the war in Ireland. First, the creation of the Solemn League and Covenant in late 1643 further sanctioned Monro's rejection of the Cessation, thus prompting the dispatch of troops under Alasdair MacColla to the Western Isles.

Second, while the withdrawal of English forces to England and Wales may have weakened opposition to the Confederation, the Cessation prevented the Irish from capitalizing on it. Third, the king was increasingly keen on negotiating a treaty with the Confederation with the sole aim of obtaining military support. Fourth, the king's defeat at Marston Moor encouraged Lord Inchiquin, commander of the Protestant forces in Munster, to change sides.[1]

Ormond, officially in charge of the negotiations, was determined to minimize any freedoms offered to the Roman Catholic population. The core of the Irish demands centred on the church, which was to be allowed complete freedom, and a restoration of church property, which would take the form of continued possession of those lands already reclaimed during the rebellion. However, the Old English were not quite as determined as their Irish allies at Kilkenny to receive open sanction for the Catholic faith: tacit acceptance would do. They were also less enthusiastic about restoring property to major exiles, such as Owen Roe O'Neill, and here they had the sympathies of some of the Irish, for both groups had benefited materially from the confiscations. Ormond sought to exploit these differences and secure a treaty along the lines of the more moderate Old English terms.[2]

While there was support for this kind of treaty, there were other pressures at work. The war in Ireland (and to some extent the wars across the British Isles) cannot be seen in a purely local context. The Irish war was regarded by many people in Ireland and on the continent, as well as by parliamentarians at Westminster, as part of the great war of the Counter-Reformation. In Europe the Thirty Years War had seen the rolling back of the Protestant Reformation and the restoration of Catholicism to parts of Germany which had become Protestant during the previous century. Now this was seen to be happening in Ireland too. Indeed, a number of Irish clerics who returned to their homeland in the wake of the rebellion were determined to ensure that this was precisely the case. With them went officers from the continental Catholic armies, such as Owen Roe O'Neill, who were determined to reverse the course of the Reformation in religious and secular terms: these men were exiles returning to their estates. Naturally, these two groups of people wanted more than the Old English and Ormond were willing to contemplate and the Vatican urged them along.

In June 1643 the representative of Pope Urban VII, Pietro Francesco Scarampi, arrived and encouraged the Irish Catholics in their demands and in 1645 the new Pope, Innocent X, sent a higher ranking representative, the nuncio Archbishop Giovanni-Battista Rinuccini, with money and weapons for the Confederation. Rinuccini enlisted the support of Owen Roe O'Neill to whom some of the weapons were sent. There were other representatives of Catholic powers in Ireland; both France and Spain, at war with each other, sent minor ranking officials to Kilkenny, where they feuded with each other and tried to exploit Ireland's role in the great religious war by recruiting Irish soldiers to fight abroad. Ireland, too, sent representatives abroad to try to persuade European states to support the war, but the continental war (and the need to retain the services of Irish troops still serving in Europe), coupled with fears of driving too great a wedge between themselves and the Westminster Parliament, kept the major powers from sending much more than good wishes and minor officials to Ireland.[3]

Attempts to defeat the Scots in Ulster had foundered by 1645. MacColla's forces in Scotland had been part of Montrose's victorious campaign which had briefly placed all Scotland in his hands (see chapters four and five) but, although the war in Scotland prevented the Edinburgh government from sending more troops into England, it had inspired the withdrawal of only 2,000 or 3,000 men from east Ulster, leaving Monro with a sizeable force. In the summer of 1644 an expedition against Monro was organized with 4,000 men added to O'Neill's Ulster army. However, because of Old English mistrust of O'Neill, who was accused of trying to win for himself the crown of Ireland, command was given to the Earl of Castlehaven. This appointment alienated O'Neill, the Marquis of Antrim and Sir Thomas Preston, each of whom wanted the command. Castlehaven was not an experienced leader – his appointment was a political one – and as a result his campaign was lacklustre. He divided his forces in the presence of the enemy, and when Monro approached in August, he was forced to withdraw and regroup. For seven weeks the army camped at Charlemont, hampered by bad weather and indecision. This was followed by a withdrawal to winter quarters. All other military action had been suspended during the campaign in order that resources could be directed towards Castlehaven's army.[4]

This was particularly unfortunate as it coincided with Inchiquin's change of heart. Charles's failure to support the Munster Protestants, coupled with the Confederation's inability to halt border incursions by some of its troops, had angered Inchiquin, who travelled to England to put his case to the king. Snubbed and denied the presidency of Munster, Inchiquin returned home. The royalist defeat at Marston Moor on 2 July 1644 convinced Inchiquin that the king might not win the war in England and Wales, and therefore that the Protestant cause would be best served by an alliance with Westminster. Inchiquin launched an offensive against the Confederation garrisons in Munster in the early autumn of 1644. It was a year before the Confederation was able to mount an effective campaign against him.

When it became clear that Ormond was not going to accede to Confederation demands, Charles sent the Earl of Glamorgan to Ireland to negotiate secretly with the Confederation in July 1645, and by August the terms had been agreed. This treaty offered far more than Ormond ever could, simply because the king was now desperate. At Naseby on June 14 his finest army had been destroyed and there was no hope of rebuilding it; by autumn 1645 the Welsh had rejected him and Montrose had been defeated in Scotland: of his kingdoms only Ireland offered hope. When Glamorgan arrived in the autumn of 1645 Rinuccini received him rather half-heartedly, principally because the treaty had been conducted secretly, and the military support

Glamorgan thought he had won never materialized because of Rinuccini's opposition. New discussions between the nuncio and Glamorgan offered more security than the earl's previous terms and the appointment of a Catholic Lord Lieutenant. By the end of the year Rinuccini thought he had secured Charles's agreement but the treaty remained secret until a copy fell into enemy hands late in the year, prompting Ormond to arrest Glamorgan for negotiating behind his back.

The public appearance of the treaty effectively killed it: the king repudiated it immediately, aware of the terrible consequences that would arise from his appearing to support the Confederation when he was not in a position of strength. Nevertheless, Glamorgan must have been able to convince Ormond that the king had sponsored his negotiations, for the earl was released in late January 1646.[5] The collapse of the secret treaty prompted urgent discussions between the Old English faction and Ormond, aimed at rescuing the king from his dire straits. But these discussions ran into Rinuccini's opposition and the public treaty agreed by the Confederation with Ormond in March 1646 was likewise rejected by the nuncio, this time because of its limited guarantees for the Catholic church; he went further, excommunicating anyone who signed it.

In the summer of 1646, the first major result of papal aid became manifest. On 5 June O'Neill's re-equipped army routed Monro at the battle of Benburb. The Scottish army was destroyed as a field force, but O'Neill failed to capitalize fully on the victory, having become embroiled in a political campaign to weaken the Old English influence on the Supreme Council. In September, with O'Neill's forces behind him, Rinuccini purged the Council of the faint-hearted.[6]

Ormond now reconsidered his own position in the light of Rinuccini's rejection of the treaty and the king's surrender at Newark, and he began to discuss handing over Dublin to the Westminster Parliament. To prevent this happening, the Confederation concentrated its efforts on a campaign against Dublin. O'Neill's Ulster army and Sir Thomas Preston's Leinster army were sent to capture Dublin, but the two never worked together (Preston was Old English) and the campaign failed; in November both armies returned to their bases. Ormond continued to discuss terms with Westminster during the first half of 1647. In June 1647 Ormond handed over Dublin to Michael Jones, son of a former Church of Ireland bishop, and to English regiments which had landed the previous month. On 8 August these forces defeated Preston at Dungan's Hill. From then on, through the autumn, Jones began to clear northern Leinster of Confederation garrisons, while in Munster Inchiquin defeated Lord Taffe's Munster army at Knocknanuss Hill on 13 November.[7]

The parliamentarians were not able to exploit their victory because they were denied the support they needed by the outbreak of war in Wales and England in May 1648 (see chapter seven). Moreover, the Scottish presence in Ulster was weakened by divided loyalty over the Engagement. Some of the Scots were sent over to England to join the Marquis of Hamilton's Engager army. However, the Confederation was also unable to repair much of the damage done or take advantage of the lull. Inchiquin had grown disillusioned with Parliament during late 1647 as the New Model Army imposed its will on Westminster, and by 20 May he had allied himself to the Confederation and proposals were laid out for an alliance with royalists, led by the Marquis of Ormond, who had discussed Irish affairs with the captive king during his brief sojourn in England. Owen Roe O'Neill on the other hand opposed the deal with Inchiquin and the royalists, withdrawing himself from the Confederation, which was now less and less under the influence of Rinuccini.

O'Neill's action effectively created a civil war within Confederation Ireland. The armies of Leinster and Inchiquin's forces were turned not on Michael Jones but on the Ulster Army, which in turn supplemented its requirement for ammunition in the autumn by negotiating with Jones to exchange beef – which Jones needed for his Leinster garrisons – for gunpowder.[8] The Confederation was in disarray, and consequently its numerical superiority and potentially superior logistics were never brought to bear on the small parliamentarian or Scottish forces on the fringes of Ireland. In late September Ormond returned to Ireland in person with the backing of a desperate king for a treaty with the Confederation. Ireland had become, once again, the centre of the king's hopes. This time Ormond had to relax his opposition to Catholic emancipation and grant toleration in the Second Ormond Peace, finalized in January 1649. A reformed army was to be created from Confederation forces, Inchiquin's army and royalist exiles. A small royalist fleet arrived at Kinsale in February 1649. By this time the king was dead (see chapter seven), and it was clear that there was renewed interest in England for settling the affairs of Ireland.[9]

SEVEN

Revolution in England and Wales

The collapse of censorship in the wake of the abolition of the Court of High Commission (see chapter three) allowed the printing industry to flourish. One effect of this was the creation of weekly or fortnightly newspapers (somewhat confusingly called diurnals or dailies because of the way in which the information was laid out under date headings like a diary). These offered great potential for propaganda and were exploited by the king's presses at Oxford and by a series of independent presses in London producing a broader spectrum of generally pro-parliamentarian newspapers. The London papers mirrored the political spectrum at London and echoed the views of the Presbyterians, the Independents and even the Scots, and thus swipes at each other accompanied attacks on the royalist presses.

The freedom of the press also allowed for a different kind of printing: tracts espousing religious and political ideas that were more radical than those coming from the pro-parliamentarian presses. The tracts questioned not only the need for a national church at all, as the Independents did, but also the nature of the baptism of infants and of accepting God's grace through free will. This created concern in many conservative circles which saw the questioning of such fundamental issues as the first step towards anarchy. The presses were also used to produce copies of petitions which were then circulated around London for signatures. These petitions, the papers and polemics had a wide circulation. Those who could not read listened to those who could, and many people became familiar with a wide range of views (even royalist papers could be found in the capital).

In this milieu grew radical movements, including religious sects such as the Baptists which had a long-standing history but had hitherto been small and dispersed, and the political group known as the Levellers. The Leveller movement was forged by radical religious thinkers like William Walwyn, who promoted religious toleration, and Richard Overton, who was angered by the intolerance of the Presbyterians, and political thinkers like John

Lilburne, who had advocated freedom of speech for Presbyterians back in the 1630s when they were persecuted and forbidden a public voice. Lilburne had the distinction of having been imprisoned by both sides by 1646: by the king in the 1630s for importing banned works by William Bastwicke and Henry Burton; by the king again in 1643 after being captured during the fighting; and in 1646 by Parliament for launching an attack on the Earl of Manchester's Presbyterianism. Even as early as 1646 the Levellers were seen as a threat. Their opponents labelled them Levellers to associate them with the destruction of property boundaries and social disintegration. Thomas Edwards was a conservative minister who believed that anarchy reigned in the Independent religious sects and political groups, and he published a catalogue of these groups' heresies both as a warning and as a guide to their recognition. He was one of the first to group Lilburne, Walwyn and Overton together as Levellers. In 1646 they certainly seemed to come together, publishing the tract *A Remonstrance of Many Thousand Citizens*, which hinted at abolishing the monarchy and the Lords, and castigated the Commons (which it suggested was the supreme political body) for betraying the people's trust. This theme was continued in the Large Petition of March 1647 which was signed by thousands of Londoners and presented to the Commons, who ordered it to be burned. At the same time, Parliament began its attack on the army.

Since the end of the war in England and Wales (except for Harlech Castle which only surrendered at about the time the Levellers handed in the Large Petition), New Model Army pay had fallen into arrears. In March 1647 the Presbyterian-dominated Parliament, which mistrusted the Independents in the army, suggested disbanding the New Model Army and drafting many of its soldiers into a new force to be sent to Ireland. This angered the unpaid soldiers, many of whom were volunteers; they could see themselves being conscripted into another war, or sent home without pay or expenses for their journey, perhaps to face lawsuits launched by vengeful royalists. In response to this, regiments of horse began to elect representatives, known as agitators, to discuss political action. The agitators circulated petitions asking for back pay, freedom from conscription for volunteers, compensation for widows and dependants, and indemnity from prosecution for actions committed while under arms, but which might otherwise be considered criminal in peacetime.

The agitators and their comrades appealed to Fairfax for help, and the army leadership was

generally supportive of the soldiers' demands.[1]
Parliament on the other hand acted with little
sensitivity, threatening to arrest soldiers bearing a
petition and announcing that the army would be
disbanded from 1 June 1647 with eight weeks' back
pay – a fraction of the total owed. At the same time
the London Trained Bands were put in a state of
defence and an *ad hoc* army created in the capital to
fend off the New Model Army should it advance on
the city. An army rendezvous was set for Newmarket,
and a troop of horse under a cornet, the lowest
ranking commissioned officer, seized the king from
Holdenby House and took him to Newmarket. It is
still not clear who urged Cornet George Joyce to do
this: some have blamed Oliver Cromwell, the
Lieutenant-General of the New Model Army, but it is
possible that Joyce was acting as the elected
representative of the soldiers he led.

The army now marched towards London, at which
Parliament became a little more conciliatory, but the
rank and file were still angry. They claimed not only
back pay and indemnity, but also that they had been
'called forth and conjured by the several
declarations of Parliament to the defence of our
own and the people's just rights and liberties . . .
and are resolved . . . to assert and vindicate the just
power and rights of this kingdom in Parliament'.[2] In

other words, men who hitherto had little, if any, stake in the political world and the government of England and Wales were asserting that because they had played a role in its defence they should have a future role in government.

As the army closed in, Parliament sent money and eleven extremely hostile members, whom the army had wanted expelled, voluntarily withdrew. London went apoplectic. Crowds of Londoners surged into Parliament demanding action against the army which they saw as the cause of their own financial difficulties. The eleven members returned and the city defences were manned. The army pressed on towards the capital and on 23 July the officers presented their own terms to the king. Now known as the *Heads of the Proposals*, these were the most liberal terms yet offered to the king: they allowed him a central role in government, and a smaller list of his supporters who would be exempt from pardon; and while they disestablished the Church of England, a Presbyterian system was not set up in its place. Moreover, Charles would have to wait for only ten years before his military powers were restored. But Charles sought only his own political advantage. He made encouraging noises about the treaty to alarm the Scots (see chapter five) and the Presbyterians in Parliament, hoping to drive a further wedge between them and the Independents. In August the army occupied London and Parliament began to deal with its pressing business, as the most vociferous Presbyterians were expelled.[3]

On 9 September Charles rejected the *Heads of the Proposals*, but many soldiers had not been satisfied with them anyway and more radical proposals were published in *The Case of the Army Truly Stated*, which also questioned the role of the army leaders, Fairfax, Cromwell and Commissary-General Henry Ireton (now labelled the Grandees) in offering such terms in the first place.[4] At around the same time, in October, the Levellers published their proposed political settlement, *The Agreement of the People*. This proposed a democratic form of government with apparently comprehensive male suffrage, with a one-chamber Parliament and no monarch.

At St Mary's church, Putney, in late October and November 1647 these ideas were discussed by the officers, the agitators and civilian Levellers. There was opposition from Cromwell and Ireton to the very notion of discussing the *Agreement* because the army was sworn to stand by the present Parliament, which the Levellers envisaged closing down. However, discussion eventually ranged widely over issues such as the franchise and the future of the king. On the former, a compromise was reached whereby a mixture of the old franchise and parliamentarian soldiers in arms before Naseby, would comprise the first electorate and the newly elected body would then establish future electorates. Some more radical members suggested that Charles, as a 'Man of Blood', be held responsible for the blood shed in the war. The 'Man of Blood' epithet was a biblical illusion and implied that the king's blood would have to be shed in order to make amends for the deaths of others. Parliament was asked not to sign a treaty with the king, although the grandees contested this decision – Ireton had stormed out during these discussions – but they were still being argued for on 11 November. A day later these discussions appeared to have fragmented the debates when dramatic news broke.

Charles had escaped from Hampton Court and made his way to Carisbrooke on the Isle of Wight. This curtailed discussions at Putney, and when several regiments defied orders and assembled at Ware to debate the *Agreement,* they were dealt with severely by Cromwell and Fairfax.[5] In what amounted almost to desperation, Parliament offered the king a new set of terms, the Four Bills, which would be the preliminary points of a settlement. At the same time Charles negotiated the Engagement with the Scots (see chapter five) and prepared for

war. On discovering the Engagement, Parliament
passed a Vote of No Addresses, suspending all
further negotiation.[6] Although the Scots were
preparing an army to invade England, renewed
fighting broke out in Wales when garrisons in
Pembrokeshire refused to disband in late February
1648. Ostensibly the rebellion began when
parliamentarian soldiers rebelled against the New
Model Army's domination of government, but the
rising was soon joined by royalists. It became a
region-wide rebellion when the leader of the rebels,
Colonel John Poyer, declared his support for the
king. Other parliamentarians under Rowland
Laugherne, who had been parliament's leading
commander in the region during the war, also went
into rebellion.[7] Parts of the New Model Army were
sent to deal with the risings. As forces left the south-
east, Kentish men and women went into rebellion at
the opening of the May assizes. Prominent at the
assizes were the Christman Rebels who had revelled
and rioted on Christmas Day 1647 in celebration of
the day, protesting at its abolition by Parliament as a
day of festivity. The Kentish rebels were joined by
some royalist officers and they seized prominent
ports and towns. On 1 June Fairfax and the
remaining part of the New Model Army defeated the
rebels at Maidstone. Surviving groups of rebels fled

north and crossed the Thames to Essex where they
joined other royalist-led rebels and, with Fairfax
bearing down on them, locked themselves into
Colchester.

On 11 July Pembroke Castle surrendered to
Cromwell, ending the rebellion in South Wales, but
by this time the Marquis of Hamilton had invaded
the north-west of England. On 27 July, after a rapid
march across England, Cromwell joined General
Lambert in Yorkshire and together they tracked the
Engager Army's slow progress through England.
Only on 17 August did Cromwell muster sufficient
forces to attack Hamilton. Having crossed the
Pennines, the New Model Army defeated the
Engager Army at Preston. Cromwell pushed down
through Lancashire, driving the remnants of
Hamilton's army into the midlands, where it
fragmented and parts of it surrendered or were
captured after skirmishes.[8] The defeat of the Scots
ended any hope of relief among the royalists in
Colchester and on 29 August they surrendered to
Fairfax. He had two of the royalist leaders shot and
sent the rest, including Lords Norwich, Capel and
Loughborough, to Windsor Castle to await trial.

With the Second Civil War over, many of the New
Model Army soldiers were in no mood for
conciliation. Charles was recognized by many as the

'Man of Blood' referred to at Putney. Presbyterians in Parliament quickly suspended the Vote of No Addresses and, in order to head off any more radical solution, reopened negotiations with the king. However, many people recognized the futility of negotiating with a king who was transparently duplicitous, and even Ireton was driven to contemplate drastic solutions to the impasse. As he negotiated with Levellers and more radical soldiers, Parliament urged the king to come to terms, but Charles was now looking towards Ormond in Ireland for help (see chapter six). Ireton and some of the soldiers suggested in the *Remonstrance of the Army* that Parliament should be purged, the negotiations ended, and the king brought to trial. Fairfax and the grandees (except for Cromwell who was in the north) initially rejected the proposals, but when their overtures to the king were again spurned the *Remonstrance* was adopted. When it was presented to Parliament, MPs set it aside without discussion. Nevertheless, the king was taken from Carisbrooke and brought to the mainland. On 6 December Colonel Thomas Pride and Lord Grey of Groby undertook a purge of the House of Commons which removed the Presbyterians and paved the way for the king's trial.

In Scotland, when news of the Engager Army's defeat arrived, there was rejoicing. In the west a radical Covenanter rising, the Wiggamore Raid, began and a march on Edinburgh organized with the aim of removing the Engager government. Although the Engagers defeated the Wiggamores, they faced a more potent threat. Cromwell and the New Model Army were marching north, having defeated George Monro and the Scottish forces drafted in from Ulster. Quickly the Wiggamores and the Engagers entered into discussions with each other. But as Cromwell approached Edinburgh in late September, the Engagers left the government and the Marquis of Argyle's faction, later known as the Kirk Party, constituted a new Committee of Estates. Assured that the Kirk party was in control, Cromwell returned south, and as the purge of Parliament took place in Westminster, he busied himself with the siege of Pontefract.[9]

On 1 January 1649 a High Court of Justice was established and the House of Lords, which opposed its creation, was suppressed. From now on the Commons regarded itself as the supreme authority, just as the Levellers had declared it to be two years earlier. By 21 January the charges and preparations were complete and the king was brought before the court. It was a show-trial with a foregone conclusion. Apart from a few hitches, including the king's refusal to recognize the court's authority and his unexpected eloquence, the trial concluded as expected, and on 27 January 1649 Charles was sentenced to death. On 30 January, outside the Banqueting Hall of Whitehall Palace, the deed was done. Before he was executed, it had been made illegal to proclaim Charles's eldest son king.[10] Over the next weeks the form of the new government was discussed. By March these discussions were over and the House of Lords and the monarchy were formally abolished. Two months later England and Wales were declared henceforth together a Commonwealth and Free State. It had been a revolution. Two of the three constituents of the old form of government, the monarchy and the aristocracy, had been swept from power. Individual aristocrats could still be involved in government, but they no longer had any automatic role. Only the House of Commons was recognized as constituting political authority in the country.[11] It was time to export the revolution.

EIGHT

Exporting the Revolution

The king was dead but the problems created during his life and reign were not. The royalists and the Catholic Confederation of Kilkenny moved towards the realization of their military ambitions in Ireland. In Scotland there was widespread anger and disbelief at the actions of the Westminster Parliament, or rather the New Model Army. Charles had been king of Scotland as well as of Ireland and England, but England, subsuming Wales, had executed Charles in the name of the English people alone. Even the hard-line Kirk Party was angered by the act. While the Scots began to look towards a working relationship with the king's heir, the Westminster Parliament set about three immediate tasks: reconstructing itself as a republican regime, removing internal opponents and dealing with Ireland.

The House of Commons declared that England and Wales were together a Commonwealth and Free State in May 1649, and a Council of State was established to replace the old privy Council and to carry out executive duties. The new government then set about creating the imagery pertaining to the state: new coats of arms for principal rooms, new maces and, where necessary, new titles for offices of state inherited from the monarchy. During the next months these symbols and forms were carried into the provinces and town corporations had coats of arms and maces produced with the badge of the Commonwealth on them.[1]

At the same time as this process of reconstruction was getting under way, a second set of measures came into operation to ensure the stability of the regime. Internal enemies in the spring of 1649 included leading royalist prisoners, held after the Second Civil War, and the Levellers. The first group were arraigned before the same High Court of Justice that had tried Charles. There was less of a foregone conclusion about these trials; Lord Capel, the Earl of Holland and the Duke of Hamilton were sentenced to death and executed, but Lord Norwich and Sir John Owen were spared. They were only the tip of a large iceberg: hundreds of less important royalists were brought before local committees all over England and in London to answer charges upon which fines and confiscations of property would be based.

The Levellers constituted an immediate and violent threat. In London dissatisfaction with the new state had led the government to prohibit discussion of politics by soldiers. This in turn had prompted John Lilburne to pen *England's New Chains Discovered*, suggesting that the tyranny of the king had been replaced by a new tyranny, that of the Council of State. It also set out new proposals for a constitution, but its principal concern was to accuse the new state of betraying the people. The Leveller paper *The Moderate* printed Lilburne's statement and called for action on important social issues, the payment of tithes to the church, unemployment and high prices, as well as calling for outstanding army pay arrears to be paid. When Fairfax and the grandees appeared hostile to the claims of the soldiers, the Levellers followed with an attack on the army leadership, accusing it, too, of betrayal. In response Lilburne, Overton, Walwyn and Thomas Prince, a party treasurer, were arrested and taken to the Tower, accused of inciting mutiny.[2]

Katherine Chidley, a leading London Leveller, and Elizabeth Lilburne, John's wife, organized petitions across the city demanding the release of the prisoners. The first petition was presented to Parliament on 25 April. It was rejected contemptuously and the women were told that they could not understand such matters. On 5 May a second petition was presented, arguing that women had equal status in the eyes of God and had an equal 'interest with the men of this nation in those liberties and securities contained in the Petition of Right and the other good laws of the land . . .'. This time the petition was signed by 10,000 women and was presented by crowds of women decked in Leveller sea-green ribbons. Once again Parliament dismissed the women and rejected the petition.[3] Other Leveller activity had already been met with state-sponsored violence. After angry discussions over pay, a minor scuffle broke out outside the Bull Inn in the city; this was termed mutiny and a 'ringleader', Robert Lockyer, was shot by firing squad. On 1 May a new version (the third) of the *Agreement of the People* was published.

The Levellers now called for another Army Council, such as that which had met at Putney, to discuss their proposals. This time their mature document called for an expanded electorate which would elect by secret ballot a 400-strong representative body, with seats distributed according to population. There was to be religious toleration and a decentralized church, and the law was similarly localized with officials appointed locally rather than nationally. When soldiers in several regiments mutinied in the midlands in support of the *Agreement*, reaction was swift. Fairfax and Cromwell attacked the main group in the village of Burford in Oxfordshire in the early hours of 15 May. Three of the rebels were executed. Defeat at Burford destroyed the Levellers' hopes of a greater role in the politics of the nation, and the movement itself, while not disappearing, nor remaining silent in the press, remained low key.

There were other radical groups in England during this period. In mid-March Fairfax had called on a group of strangers encamped on land at St George's Hill, London. This group had begun to till and sow waste ground. They called themselves the True Levellers, but are better known as the Diggers. In their pamphlet *The True Levellers Standard Advanced*, the leading figures, Gerard Winstanley and William Everard, claimed that God had given the earth to all humans to be shared equally, and that all should share in its bounty by virtue of working the land. There were few Diggers at St George's, but there were other colonies in the south and east midlands. While their numbers were small and Fairfax had regarded them as mad rather than dangerous, landowners in the vicinity of the colonies reacted angrily and violently. The Diggers proclaimed that quietly and through example they would show that property-holding defied God's word. This threatened the basis of wealth and power, as property was the paramount means of acquiring both. Landowners were fearful that, in those times of high prices and widespread unemployment, the Diggers might attract landless labourers and the dispossessed, and used armed gangs and the courts to destroy the colonies. Within eighteen months they seem to have all gone.[4]

Religious sects also angered many people during the early months of the Republic. Groups such as the Ranters were developing out of the intense period of questioning about which Thomas Edwards had been so upset in the mid-1640s. The Ranters believed that there was no such thing as sin and that as God had created all acts and actions, so they were all godly things. This allowed for overturning gender and sexual mores among other things, and thus the Ranters became associated with sexual promiscuity. Although few in number, the Ranters attracted attention in the press and pulpit. Many Ranters moved on to other sects during the 1650s. None of these small groups, no matter how much they excited the spleen of commentators, posed the same threat as the Levellers, and their roles as 'enemies within' were correspondingly very minor.[5]

The Commonwealth turned its attention to Ireland very soon after Burford. Ireland's coat of arms was included in the Commonwealth's emblem, signalling that it was to be regarded as a subordinate possession of the English polity as the Irish kingdom had been under the monarchy. Moreover, Ireland's role in the continental wars (where most fighting had ended in 1648), and its ties to Catholic European powers (see chapter six), meant that it could be regarded as a strategic liability, open to foreign intervention. Royalist ships were also using Irish ports as bases for attacking Commonwealth shipping. As a result the reconquest of Ireland and the defeat of the Confederation/royalist alliance had a very high priority.

A major blow in the renewed war had been delivered before Cromwell and the New Model Army could be dispatched. Ormond had assembled a large composite army and surrounded Dublin. His army was composed of people who had been on opposite sides earlier in the war, Preston and Inchiquin being the principal two. As a result coordination was poor, and Michael Jones was able to take advantage of this on 2 August when he defeated Ormond at Rathmines. This cleared the Dublin hinterland, and a fortnight later Cromwell landed. The New Model Army marched northwards and attacked Drogheda. General O'Neill had refused to rejoin the Confederation since the previous year and, although he negotiated with Ormond, he also tried to contact Westminster.

The defeat at Rathmines dashed any chance of discussions with the English, and help from European powers was unlikely so O'Neill began negotiations about joining Ormond's coalition. However, O'Neill could do little to stop Cromwell: he had fallen ill and could not lead an attack on the New Model Army. Ormond was still recovering from his defeat, and on 11 September Drogheda was stormed. Many soldiers and civilians were killed in the fighting and the aftermath. Cromwell concocted a series of lame excuses for the butchery, centring on retribution for the 1641/2 massacres which had already acquired mythical status. He ignored the fact that Drogheda had at the time been in Protestant hands, and had only recently become part of the coalition. Cromwell's real motives probably lay in a desire to enact brutal victories to cow other garrisons into early surrender. After Drogheda he turned south to Wexford, a major base for royalist shipping.

On 12 October, Owen Roe O'Neill, now dying, joined the coalition, and Cromwell stormed Wexford. Once again there was a massacre of soldiers and civilians both during and after the fighting, and again Cromwell claimed that the dead were tainted by blood-guilt for the massacres of 1641. In fact, Wexford people had been only marginally if at all involved in the murders of 1641. But Cromwell's savagery had the desired effect of impelling some garrisons to surrender: Ross did so by 20 October. Waterford, however, remained defiant and the New Model Army had to press on along the south coast. Despite the outbreak of plague among the soldiery, which claimed the life of Michael Jones, the New Model Army took control of much of Munster during the winter of 1649/50. In the spring Cromwell's force moved north to Tipperary and then back to Leinster where Kilkenny fell to him on 28 March. With defeat of the Munster forces and the fall of Clonmel in April, resistance in the south and east of Ireland was almost at an end. On 21 June 1650, at Scariffhollis in Donegal, the Ulster Army, led since O'Neill's death by the Bishop of Clogher, was defeated by Sir Charles Coote. The focus of the war switched to Connacht, where resistance was to continue for many months.[6]

On 26 May 1650 Cromwell returned to Britain, leaving his son-in-law Henry Ireton to continue the work in Ireland. By this time the anger of the Scots had made the Kirk Party throw in its lot with Prince

Charles, who had already appointed the Marquis of Montrose Lieutenant-General of Scotland and authorized him to land mercenaries on the Scottish coast. But as soon as Edinburgh made approaches to Charles, to secure the aid of the Scots he had to repudiate Montrose. When his small army was defeated at Carbisdale on 27 April, the royalist general was captured, and was tried and executed in Edinburgh in May. Charles had to fulfil two other conditions: firstly, to repudiate his allies in Ireland (because of the treaty with the Catholic Confederation) and, secondly, to sign the Covenant. Even so, the Marquis of Argyle and the Kirk Party were keen to exclude the prince from power, and the creation of their new army was to be undertaken without support from former royalists or Engagers. Charles was not to have any command in this army, nor was he to be crowned. The army was placed under the command of the Covenanter hero David Leslie, who attempted to deny the invading New Model Army resources when it entered Scotland in late July 1650 under Cromwell.

Lord Fairfax, whose acceptance of the king's execution and the imposition of the republic had been grudging, refused to lead the army against the Scots and had gone into retirement, and Cromwell was appointed commander-in-chief in his place. By

27 July he had reached Dunbar, but illness among the troops and lack of resources reduced the effectiveness of his invasion. Leslie moved against the New Model Army on 2 September, hoping to trap and destroy it just south of Dunbar. However, on the following day Cromwell defeated the Scots army. Disease among the English and Welsh soldiers prevented the campaign being concluded and left time for the Scots to forge a new army. Although Cromwell captured south-east Scotland and took Edinburgh, the Scots did not concede. A power-shift brought on by the defeat now took place in Scotland and Charles was proclaimed king. A new army was created with royalist and Engager recruits. This was a compromise which split the Covenanter political world into those who accepted the treaty with the new king (the Resolutioners), and those who demanded the purity of the Covenanter cause (the Protestors). As this new army was created, Cromwell languished in illness, and General Lambert proved unable to shift the Scots from the defensive line Leslie had established between the Forth and the Clyde.

When Cromwell returned to health in June 1651, attempts were made to attack the centre and east of the Scots lines. This concentration weakened the Commonwealth forces in western Scotland and the adjacent borders. Charles and the Scots seized their chance and invaded England. By 10 August Charles's army had reached Wigan, but the reception in England was disappointing. The Republic had been accepted by the majority of people, even if only as a means by which the years of warfare were ended, and renewed fighting was clearly unwanted. Charles was joined by only about 100 English soldiers during his march. He tried to establish a major city base, but was turned away from Shrewsbury and Gloucester; finally, in late August, Worcester opened its gates to the invaders. After the capture of Stirling, Cromwell turned his army round and followed Charles into England, and by 3 September the New Model Army and local levies had arrived outside Worcester. The Scots and royalists were trapped in the town as the encircling Commonwealth army moved in. A break-out by royalist horse halted the approach for a short time, but in the end, Charles was forced to abandon his army and begin a long game of cat-and-mouse with government forces before escaping to France.[7]

Cromwell referred to the battle of Worcester as 'a crowning mercy' which had secured the safety of the Republic. The wars in Ireland and Scotland continued into 1653, but after Scariffhollis, Dunbar and Worcester, these were minor skirmishes concerned with eradicating already defeated enemies. The Republic now turned its military strength towards war with the United Provinces over international trade. Early in 1652 the Scottish political élite was presented with a choice: accept a political union with the Commonwealth or be treated as a conquered nation. For Ireland there had been no such choice: the defeated Confederation politicians had been apostate because of their religion. The Scots acceded. The hard-won fruits of the political revolution of 1639–41 were swept away. The independent executive in the form of the Committee of Estates, and the powerful legislative, the Estates, both of which had been models for the English and Welsh revolutions of 1640–2 and 1649, were abolished, along with the General Assembly. The division of 1650 between the Resolutioners and the Protesters had so weakened the Scottish political and religious world that no opposition could be mounted to counter Commonwealth pressure. Scotland was to be represented at Westminster, but many of its representatives turned out to be Englishmen from the army of occupation, or political placemen.

The same was to be true of Ireland. There a new land settlement was being put in place which confirmed the status of Ireland as a colonial dependency. Catholic Irish families from Munster, Leinster and Ulster, who were not entirely dispossessed because of their involvement with the Confederation, were to be deprived of their estates and given lands worth one-third of those estates in Connacht. The Catholic population was thus largely deprived of its links with politics in the country. By the time the first representatives of the newly incorporated countries arrived at Westminster, the republican world had changed again.

The Westminster Parliament had made great strides towards establishing the republican regime, but it struggled with finances, just as the Parliament it had grown out of had done. Taxation was still heavy in the early years of the 1650s, and yet the army was still in arrears by 1653. Fears that the army would not be fully compensated by this assembly or by its proposed successor led to angry exchanges between politicians and the military. On 20 April Cromwell and a body of armed men entered Parliament and expelled the assembly. In its place a Council of State ruled until a new nominated assembly, effectively the first Parliament of the British Isles, assembled on 4 July 1653. This was the short-lived Little Parliament, disparagingly referred to as Barebones's Parliament after Praise-God Barebones, one of its members. One faction, alarmed by Parliament's failure to deal effectively either with the war against the Dutch or with army finances, forced the dissolution of the house on 12 December. Before the end of the year a new constitution, the Instrument of Government, was in place, establishing the Protectorate, with Oliver Cromwell as Lord Protector at its head, a Council of State as the executive, and a Parliament of the four nations as its legislative. The Protectorate remained in being until February 1659.[8]

Between 1637 and 1653 the four nations of the British Isles underwent a series of revolutions and wars which did much to change the form of society in each country. The rebellion in Scotland generated a war in which defeat left Charles powerless in the face of a political revolution in Scotland, and then in England and Wales. In turn these engendered rebellion in Ireland, which created the conditions for civil war in England. The duplicity of Charles I after his defeat in this war drove wedges between the allied nations of Scotland and England and Wales, leaving England and Wales free to enact a more fundamental revolution which resulted in the execution of the king. Empowered by the freedom from internal strife, England and Wales were then able to complete the defeat of the Confederation of Kilkenny and to take on and defeat their estranged former ally Scotland. By 1653 the four nations were united more closely than they had ever been, but the unification had involved a great deal of coercion on the part of England and Wales, and thus did not enjoy the willing cooperation of many Scots and Irish people. Moreover, the revolution did not go far enough to secure the affections of the majority of people: it did not, for instance, deal satisfactorily with the issue of tithes, and it was helpless in the face of high unemployment. True, the political framework of each nation had been fundamentally altered, but the basis for power had never been widened much beyond the limited franchises on offer in the four nations in 1637.

The narrowness of control at the top, forced on the Protectorate by the fragile nature of its construction out of the competing claims of the army and civilian power-brokers in 1653, meant that a good deal of time was needed for deeper issues to be resolved. There was also another problem: the keystone position of Oliver Cromwell, the chief powerbroker in 1653. Cromwell's untimely death in 1658 plunged the Protectorate into a downward spiral of instability from which it could only have escaped if the powerbase were more widely secured. The new state had certainly done much to foster support among the people – taxes were lowered throughout the mid- to late 1650s, and law was practised in English which, in England at least, could be understood by the people, rather than by only a few Latin-educated people – but the people had not been fully absorbed into the process of change that a true revolution requires to stand. In 1653 the collapse of the Republic was unforeseen, but the opportunities offered by some Leveller ideas on representation, by the re-creation of the state, had already been rejected, and the narrow and ultimately unstable hierarchy was already in place. The civil wars were over, but the political wars were not. The remainder of the 1650s saw these political wars rock the Protectorate and ultimately, in 1659, tear it apart.

Notes

CHAPTER ONE

1. For discussions of these aspects of Charles's rule see M. Lee, *The Road to Revolution, Scotland under Charles I 1625–1637* (Chicago, University of Illinois Press, 1985).
2. J. Morrill, *The Nature of the English Revolution* (London, Longman, 1993), pp. 92–3.
3. D.H. Fleming (ed.), 'Scotland's Supplication and Complaint against the Book of Common Prayer (otherwise Laud's Liturgy), the Book of Canons and the Prelates', *Proceedings of the Society of Antiquaries of Scotland*, LX (1923), 371–3.
4. Morrill, *The English Revolution*, pp. 104–5.
5. A.L. MacInnes, *Charles I and the Making of the Covenanting Movement* (Edinburgh, John Donald, 1991), pp. 166–8.
6. Ibid., pp. 185–6.
7. M. Fissel, *The Bishops' Wars* (Cambridge, Cambridge University Press, 1994), pp. 26–8.
8. MacInnes, *Charles I and the Covenanting Movement*, p. 194.
9. Fissel, *The Bishops' Wars*, pp. 53–60.
10. M. Bennett, *The Civil Wars in Britain and Ireland, 1637–1651* (Oxford, Blackwell, 1997), pp. 87–90.

CHAPTER TWO

1. For an important discussion of this government see H.F.

Kearney, *Strafford in Ireland, 1633–1641: A Study in Absolutism*, rev. edn (Cambridge, Cambridge University Press, 1989).

2. Bennett, *The Civil Wars*, pp. 36–8.
3. D. Stevenson, *Highland Warrior: Alisdair MacColla and the Civil Wars* (Edinburgh, Edinburgh University Press, 1994), pp. 64–5.
4. M. Perceval-Maxwell, *The Outbreak of the Irish Rebellion of 1641* (Dublin, Gill and Macmillan, 1994), p. 78.
5. Bennett, *The Civil Wars*, p. 9.
6. *Calendar of State Papers Relating to Ireland, 1633–1647* (London, HMSO, 1901), pp. 333–4.
7. Perceval-Maxwell, *The Outbreak of the Irish Rebellion*, pp. 104–5.
8. J.I. Casaway, *Owen Roe O'Neill and the Struggle for Catholic Ireland* (Philadelphia, University of Pennsylvania Press, 1984), pp. 46–9.

CHAPTER THREE

1. One of the most recent of such criticisms has been K. Sharpe, *The Personal Rule of Charles I* (New Haven, Yale University Press, 1992).
2. Fissel, *The Bishops' Wars*, pp. 264–6, 270.
3. Bennett, *The Civil Wars*, pp. 56–7.
4. Fissel, *The Bishops' Wars*, pp. 54–60.
5. C. Russell, *The Fall of the British Monarchies* (Oxford, Oxford University Press, 1991), p. 149.
6. Ibid., pp. 229–31.
7. Bennett, *The Civil Wars*, pp. 77–81.
8. Earl of Clarendon, *The History of the Rebellion and Civil Wars in England*, repr. (Oxford, Oxford University Press, 1992), vol. I, pp. 421–4.
9. B. Manning, *The English People and the English Revolution* (London, Heinemann, 1976), pp. 84–92.

#CHAPTER FOUR

1. J. Ohlmeyer (ed.), *Ireland: From Independence to Occupation* (Cambridge, Cambridge University Press, 1995), pp. 44–5.
2. Ibid., pp. 46–7.
3. The best description of this process is to be found in A. Fletcher, *The Outbreak of the English Civil War* (London, Arnold, 1981), particularly chapter eleven.
4. Bennett, *The Civil Wars*, pp. 160–4.
5. Ibid., pp. 207–8.
6. J.P. Kenyon, *The Civil Wars of England* (London, Weidenfield and Nicholson, 1989), p. 113.
7. The best account of this process is to be found in I. Gentles, *The New Model Army in England, Ireland and Scotland* (Oxford, Blackwell, 1992).
8. The best account of the wars in Scotland is to be found in Stevenson, *Highland Warrior*, chapters five to seven.

CHAPTER FIVE

1. See Stevenson, *Highland Warrior*, pp. 206–11.
2. Ibid. Chapter nine is the best account of this campaign.
3. D. Stevenson, *Revolution and Counter Revolution in Scotland* (London, Royal Historical Society, 1977), pp. 55–9.
4. Bennett, *The Civil Wars*, pp. 277–9.
5. G. Aylmer, *The Levellers in the English Revolution* (London, Thames and Hudson, 1975), p. 29.
6. S.R. Gardiner, *History of the Great Civil War* (originally published 1893; Adelstrop, Windrush Press, 1987), pp. 100–1.

CHAPTER SIX

1. Ohlmeyer, *From Independence to Occupation*, pp. 48–50.
2. J. Casaway, *Owen Roe O'Neill*, pp. 89–90.
3. See Ohlmeyer, *From Independence to Occupation*, chapter five for a good discussion of Ireland in the European sphere.
4. Ibid., pp. 51–2; Casaway, *Owen Roe O'Neill*, pp. 103–12.
5. Bennett, *The Civil Wars*, pp. 251–3.
6. Ohlmeyer, *From Independence to Occupation*, pp. 54–5.
7. Ibid., pp. 55–7.
8. Casaway, *Owen Roe O'Neill*, pp. 210–16.
9. Ibid., pp. 251–2.

CHAPTER SEVEN

1. Gentles, *The New Model Army*, pp. 148–51.
2. Kenyon, *The Civil Wars*, p. 167.
3. Ibid., p. 170.
4. Aylmer, *The Levellers*, p. 29.
5. G. Aylmer, *Rebellion or Revolution: England from Civil War to Restoration* (Oxford, Oxford University Press, 1986), p. 90.
6. S.R. Gardiner, *History of the Great Civil War*, vol. 4, pp. 50–2.
7. Ibid., p. 112.
8. Kenyon, *The Civil Wars*, p. 189.
9. Bennett, *The Civil Wars*, pp. 303–5.
10. See C.V. Wedgwood, *The Trial of Charles I* (originally published 1964; Harmondsworth, Penguin, 1983), for details of the trial.
11. R. Hutton, *The British Republic* (London, Longman, 1990), p. 4.

CHAPTER EIGHT

1. For recent work on this theme see S. Kelsey, *Inventing a Republic: The Political Culture of the English Commonwealth, 1649–1653* (Manchester, Manchester University Press, 1997).
2. Aylmer, *The Levellers*, pp. 142–3.
3. B. Manning, *1649: The Crisis of the English Revolution* (London, Bookmarks, 1992), pp. 157–63.
4. Ibid., pp. 123–4.
5. Bennett, *The Civil Wars*, pp. 356–9.
6. Ohlmeyer, *From Independence to Occupation*, pp. 61–3.
7. R. Mitchison, *Lordship to Patronage: Scotland 1603–1745* (originally published 1983; Edinburgh, Edinburgh University Press, 1990), pp. 60–3.
8. Hutton, *The British Republic*, pp. 60–2.

Further Reading

PRINTED PRIMARY SOURCES

For those wishing to examine the history of this period using some of the original sources, the best place to start is with printed volumes. There are many collections of printed papers, from diaries through to government papers. It is essential that the reader has a good grounding in secondary sources to enable the documents to be set into context. Official papers can be found in the series of volumes called *Calendar of State Papers: Domestic, Charles I* (Liechtenstein, Kraus reprint, 1967) and for Irish affairs similar documents can be found in the *Calendar of State Papers Relating to the Reign of Charles I, 1633–47* (London, HMSO, 1901) and *Calendar of State Papers Relating to Ireland in the Reign of Charles I, 1647–1660* (London, HMSO, 1903).

One of the most readable near-contemporary histories is the Earl of Clarendon's *The History of the Rebellion and Civil Wars in England*, edited by W.H. Mackay (Oxford, Clarendon Press, 1888, republished in paperback in 1992). Clarendon, then Sir Edward Hyde, was an advisor to Charles I from 1641. He later worked for Charles II during the interregnum, and during the Restoration. He can therefore in some cases give first-hand accounts of the period and the character portraits that enliven his text often sparkle because he knew them personally. For Scottish history, a good starting point is the selection of documents found in *A Source Book of Scottish History, 1567–1707*, vol. three, edited by W.C. Dickinson and G. Donaldson (Edinburgh, Nelson, 1954). For those wishing to savour the depth of religious feeling in 1637 then D.H. Fleming's article 'Scotland's Supplication and Complaint against the Book of Common Prayer (otherwise Laud's Liturgy), the Book of Canons and the Prelates' in the *Proceedings of the Society of the Antiquaries of Scotland*, vol. LX (1923) makes good reading. Irish affairs can be found in the three volumes edited by J.T. Gilbert, *A Contemporary History of Affairs in Ireland from 1641–1652* (Dublin, Irish Archaeological and Celtic Society, 1879–80). The diary of the Scottish lawyer Archibald Johnston, edited by G.H. Paul, D.H. Fleming and J.D. Ogilvie, and published in three volumes as the *Diary of Sir Archibald Johnston of Wariston* (Edinburgh, Scottish History Society, 1911, 1919, 1940), gives a fascinating insight into the mental world of one of the king's leading opponents. The first volume deals with the period when opposition to the king was developing and is particularly interesting as Johnston tries to reconcile his action with the will of God.

SECONDARY SOURCES

There are many general texts which cover the period 1637–1653 in whole or in part, two of the most recent being M. Bennett's *The Civil Wars in Britain and Ireland, 1637–1651* (Oxford, Blackwell, 1997) and also his briefer study *The English Civil War* (London, Longman, 1995). For very detailed nineteenth-century histories, the works of S.R. Gardiner, *A History of the Great Civil War* in four volumes (originally publ. 1893; Adelstrop, Windrush Press, 1987) and *A History of the Commonwealth and Protectorate, 1649–1656* (originally publ. 1903; Adelstrop, Windrush Press,

1988) are still valuable works of reference. Dame C.V. Wedgwood's narrative histories, *The King's Peace* (originally publ. 1955; Harmondsworth, Penguin, 1983), *The King's War* (originally publ. 1958; Harmondsworth, Penguin, 1983) and her *Trial of Charles I* (originally publ. 1964; Harmondsworth, Penguin, 1983) still provide absorbing reading and continue Gardiner's tradition of examining the war across the British Isles. J.P. Kenyon's *The Civil Wars of England* (London, Weidenfeld and Nicholson, 1989) asks interesting questions about the way the war was fought and provides a fast-moving narrative of the war, but it fails to explore the wider political and social issues. David Stevenson's two works, *The Scottish Revolution, 1637–44* (Newton Abbot, David and Charles, 1973) and *Revolution and Counter-Revolution in Scotland, 1644–1651* (London, Royal Historical Society, 1977), together present an excellent examination of Scottish history during the period. The collection of essays in Jane Ohlmeyer's *Ireland, From Independence to Occupation, 1641–60* (Cambridge, Cambridge University Press, 1995) cover this same period of Irish history. For a background to Welsh history in the seventeenth century, see G. Williams's *Renewal and Reformation: Wales, c. 1415–1642* (Oxford, Oxford University Press, 1993).

Gerald Aylmer, in *Rebellion or Revolution: England from Civil War to Restoration* (Oxford, Oxford University Press, 1986), provides an excellent analysis of the period and tries to establish the nature of these dramatic years. His work on one of the radical political groups, *The Levellers in the English Revolution* (London, Thames and Hudson, 1975), remains a good starting point for examining the Levellers through their own words. John Morrill's collection of essays, *The Nature of the English Revolution* (London, Longman, 1993), also attempts to answer similar questions to Aylmer's *Rebellion or Revolution*, and shows the development of the author's thoughts over the years. Christopher Hill still provides the best and most readable attempts at a Marxist analysis of the period in works such as: *God's Englishman, Oliver Cromwell and the English Revolution* (originally publ. 1970; Harmondsworth, Penguin, 1979), *The English Revolution* (originally publ. 1940; London, Lawrence and Wishart, 1979) and *The World turned Upside Down* (originally publ. 1972; Harmondsworth, Penguin, 1975). Brian Manning's political analysis of the role of ordinary people, *The English People and the English Revolution, 1640–1649* (London, Heinemann, 1976), still makes an important contribution to discussion, but his *1649: The Crisis of the English Revolution* (London, Bookmarks, 1992) is an excellent attempt to examine the wide range of influence that the revolution had on people's lives. Charles Carlton, in *Going to the Wars: The Experience of the British Civil Wars, 1638–1651* (London, Routledge, 1992), attempts to explore the lives of ordinary soldiers from enlistment to death or survival during the wars in a fascinating study. Ian Gentles, in *The New Model Army in England, Ireland and Scotland, 1645–1653* (Oxford, Blackwell, 1992), explores the development of the most famous army of the period and looks at its increasing political awareness. Perhaps the best study of the way in which royalists fought the war is Ronald Hutton's *The Royalist War Effort* (London, Longman, 1982); unfortunately no similar study of royalist organization in other regions is in print.

The reasons for the civil wars have been recently discussed by Conrad Russell in *The Causes of the English Civil War* (Oxford, Oxford University Press, 1990) and in far more detail in *The Fall of the British Monarchies, 1632–42* (Oxford, Oxford University Press, 1991). Both of Russell's works are essentially political explanations for the war, but they do successfully incorporate the four nations. A wider context for Russell's revisionist stance can be obtained by reading Kevin Sharpe's *The Personal Rule of Charles I* (New Haven, Yale University Press, 1992). However, Ann Hughes's brief volume, *The Causes of the English Civil War* (London, Longman, 1992), contains a much broader and well-thought-out analysis, tackling some of Russell's presumptions about the political causes of the civil war. The same period from a Scottish perspective is covered in M. Lee's *The Road to Revolution, Scotland under Charles I, 1625–1637* (Chicago, University of Illinois Press, 1985), A.I. MacInnes's *Charles I and the Making of the Covenanting Movement, 1625–1641* (Edinburgh, John Donald, 1991) and P. Donald's *An Uncouncilled King; Charles I and the Scottish Troubles, 1637–41* (Cambridge, Cambridge University Press, 1990), each in very different ways, while K.M. Brown's *Kingdom or Province: Scotland and the Regal Union* (London, Macmillan, 1992) sets this into the broader context of the relationship between Scotland and England during the seventeenth century. Works by Jenny Wormald, including *Scotland Revisited* (London, Collins and Brown, 1991) and *Court, Kirk and Community* (London, Edward Arnold, 1981) provide a good historical context.

The same service for Ireland is undertaken by Nicholas Canny in *From Reformation to Restoration, Ireland 1534–1660* (Dublin, Helicon, 1987), while H.F. Kearney's *Strafford in Ireland, 1633–1641: A Study in Absolutism* (originally publ. 1959; Cambridge, Cambridge University Press, 1989) puts the rebellion into the context of the government of Ireland during the 1630s. M. Perceval-Maxwell's *The Outbreak of the Irish Rebellion of 1641* (Dublin, Gill and Macmillan, 1994) provides a detailed political analysis of the rebellion in Ireland, although a wider social analysis is provided in the collection of essays found in

FURTHER READING

Ulster 1641, Aspects of the Rising, edited by B. Mac Cuarta (Belfast, Institute of Irish Studies, 1993). Jane Ohlmeyer's *Civil War and Restoration in the Three Stuart Kingdoms. The Career of Randal MacDonnell, Marquis of Antrim, 1609–1683* (Cambridge, Cambridge University Press, 1993) examines the wars in the context of the Marquis of Antrim, a man with political and economic interests across the British Isles.

The outbreak of warfare is covered in Mark Fissel's excellent study of the 1639 and 1640 wars, *The Bishops' Wars: Charles I's Campaigns against Scotland* (Cambridge, Cambridge University Press, 1994), and Anthony Fletcher's *The Outbreak of the English Civil War* (London, Arnold, 1981) is an unsurpassed overall study of the descent into war in England and Wales in 1642. The war in Scotland is covered in David Stevenson's *Highland Warrior: Alasdair MacColla and the Civil Wars* (originally publ. 1980; Edinburgh, Saltire Society, 1994), which examines the fighting from the perspective of MacColla and the ambitions of the MacDonald clan; this can be read in conjunction with Jane Ohlmeyer's study of the clan chief, Antrim. The war in Ireland is explained in a similar way by Jerrold Casaway's *Owen Roe O'Neill and the Struggle for Catholic Ireland* (Philadelphia, University of Pennsylvania Press, 1984). John Morrill looks at the way in which the war was perceived by many of those people who lived through it in *The Revolt of the Provinces* (London, Longman, 1976) and with other authors in *Reactions to the English Civil War* (London, Macmillan, 1982) and *The Impact of the English Civil War* (London, Collins and Brown, 1991) both of which he edited. In *Revel, Riot and Rebellion: Popular Politics and Culture in England, 1603–60* (Oxford, Clarendon Press, 1985) David Underdown examines popular involvement in the war in the south-west of England.

The Republic has come in for renewed discussion in a series of works, and Ronald Hutton's *The British Republic* (London, Macmillan, 1990) makes an excellent starting point. R. Hainsworth's *The Swordsmen in Power: War and Politics under the English Republic, 1649–1660* (Stroud, Sutton, 1997) is a mine of information if somewhat densely detailed. Sean Kelsey's *Inventing a Republic: the Political Culture of the English Commonwealth, 1649–1653* (Manchester, Manchester University Press, 1997) is an interesting attempt to argue that we should not necessarily see the Commonwealth period (1649–53) as leading inevitably towards the Protectorate. John Morrill and a series of authors continue the attempt to analyse a broad perspective of the period's history, begun with *The Impact of the English Civil War*, in *Revolution and Restoration: England in the 1650s* (London, Collins and Brown, 1992).

Index

Jones, Michael 68, 70, 90, 92

Kilsyth 48, 50, 51
Knocknanuss Hill 69

Lambert, General 80, 94
Langport 48
Large Petition 73–4
Laud, Abp William 25, 28, 30, 31
Laugherne, Rowland 79
Leicester 48
Leicester, Earl of 20
Leslie, Sir Alexander 9
Leslie, David 45, 51–2, 55–6, 93, 94
Levellers 57, 72–3, 77, 81, 85, 86–8, 100
Lilburne, Elizabeth 86
Lilburne, John 72–3, 86
London 15, 33–4, 71, 74, 75–7, 86, 88; Treaty of 32
Lostwithiel 44

MacColla, Alasdair 46, 47, 50, 51, 52, 55, 56, 61, 64
Maidstone 79
Manchester, Earl of 42–3, 44, 45, 73
Marston Moor 43–4, 62, 66
Maurice, Prince 40
Militia Bill 37
Monro, George 82
Monro, Robert 35, 39, 61, 65, 68
Montrose, Earl (Marquis) of 8, 11, 47–8, 49, 50, 51–2, 53, 64, 66, 93

Nantwich 42
Naseby 48, 66
National Covenant 6–7, 8, 16
Negative Confession 6–7

New Model Army 46, 48, 56, 69, 74–5, 79, 80, 82, 84, 90–1, 92, 93, 94, 95
Newark 43, 52, 53–4, 68
Newburn 10, 30
Newbury 42, 44, 46
Newcastle, Earl (Marquis) of 40, 41, 42, 43–4
newspapers 37, 71

O'Neill, Owen Roe 21, 61, 62, 63, 65, 68, 69–70, 91
Ormond, Earl (Marquis) of 13, 22, 35, 39, 40, 59, 62, 63, 66, 67, 68, 69, 70, 81, 90–1
Overton, Richard 72, 73, 86
Oxford 43, 44, 48, 71

Pacification of Berwick 9, 28
Parliament: House of Commons 45, 81, 82, 83, 84–5; House of Lords 46, 82, 83; Little (Barebones) 97; Long 20; Short 30; Vote of No Addresses 79, 81
Petition of Right 24, 29
Philliphaugh 51
Plymouth 40, 42
Pointz, Sydenham 53
Pontefract 82
Poyning's Law 20
Presbyterians 3, 14, 45, 54, 58, 71, 72, 73, 74, 76, 77, 81
Preston 80
Preston, Sir Thomas 65, 68–9, 90
Pride, Colonel Thomas 81
printing industry 71–2
Protectorate 98–100
Pym, John 29, 33, 41

Ranters 89
Rathmines 90, 91

Rinuccini, Abp Giovanni–Battista 64, 66–7, 68, 69
Rupert, Prince 43

Scarampi, Pietro Francesco 63–4
Scotland (Scots) 1–11, 14, 16, 27, 40–1, 42, 45, 46–8, 50–60, 61, 64–5, 68, 71, 81–2, 84, 92–6, 98, 99
Selby 42
Ship Money 24, 25, 26, 29, 31
Solemn League and Covenant 41, 47, 61; Army of the 41, 42, 51, 52–3, 55
Stow-on-the-Wold 53
Strafford, Earl of (Sir Thomas Wentworth) 14–20, 31, 32

Ten Propositions 32
Trained Bands 28, 29–30, 37, 75
Triennial Act 11, 32
Turnham Green 38

Ulster 12–13, 14, 15, 16, 21–2, 35, 39, 40, 60, 61, 64–5, 68, 69, 70, 97
United Provinces 96, 98
Ussher, Abp James 15

Wales (Welsh) 13, 14, 23, 27, 28, 37, 38, 39, 40, 41, 42, 45, 49, 53, 54, 57, 58, 66, 69, 70, 74, 80, 83, 84, 98, 99
Waller, Sir William 43, 44
Walwyn, William 72, 73, 86
Wandesworth, Sir Christopher 18, 19
Wiggamore Raid 82
Worcester 38, 95